# Getting Started

## A Preface to Writing

# Getting
# Started

## A Preface to Writing

HARRY ROUGIER AND

E. KRAGE STOCKUM

UNIVERSITY OF DAYTON

W · W · NORTON & COMPANY · INC
NEW YORK

SBN 393 09900 8
Library of Congress Catalog Card No. 79-98889
Printed in the United States of America
2 3 4 5 6 7 8 9 0

# Contents

# Preface

Before we began writing this book, we talked for months about the college student-writer and the kind of help he needs. As we see him, he is one who has had innumerable experiences, both real and vicarious; who is educated and knowledgeable; who recognizes the value of the individual man and yet sees men as brothers and the experience of mankind as universal; who instinctively trusts his own feelings; who wants to share what he knows and feels.

Ironically, he, who has much to say, has difficulty finding subjects on which he can write something true to himself and relevant to readers whose lives are as individual as his own. And he has difficulty writing—translating his thoughts linearly, into words, sentences, and paragraphs that will re-translate into precisely those thoughts in the mind and heart of a reader who may not already share them, a reader he does not know and cannot see.

We wrote this book to help you find your own way through both difficulties: to help you sort through your stored knowledge and experience for your own best subjects; to help you during the act of thinking through and putting down what you need and want to say, to bring about in your reader the effect you intend.

In Chapter One, we examine those abilities you apply in common to talking and writing, and then we make a distinction between the two as communication, with emphasis on the difference between listener and reader. We show how you can develop a hypothetical reader that you can depend on to tell you when your writing is "coming through" and when it is not.

Chapters Two and Three concentrate upon the mind at work with the materials of writing. In these chapters you will find numerous ways of developing insights and evolving theses from knowledge and ideas you already have. We show you how other writers have dealt with the same problems you meet in your writing. The diagrams, samples, and experiments will help you work out on your own a number of ways to think through your writing.

The subject of Chapter Four is the literal, physical job of writing—what to do once you have clearly in mind what you are going to write about. We give you suggestions for making efficient use of the time you spend writing. Hundreds of good writers have used these techniques; there is no reason you should not make your job easier by adopting some of them. We included a section on how to avoid what we call the bog-down—and after it a section on what to do if, in spite of everything, you do bog down.

Because we know that writing is a very personal thing, nowhere in the book do we imply, "This is the way you should write because it has always been the way" or even "This is the best way because it has always been the best." We offer instead, "This is a good way because it works, usually, and may well work for you in any number of particular cases; and this is another good way; and so is this, and so is this."

Harry Rougier
E. Krage Stockum

# Getting Started

A Preface to Writing

# CHAPTER ONE

# Talking and Writing

## Using Audience Signals

### RESPONDING TO VISUAL SIGNALS

You are with four friends. They are discussing a subject that interests you, but thus far you have been only listening. Quite without warning, they ask for your opinion. Suddenly, all eyes are on you.

Under this pressure, you are forced to make an immediate statement or refuse to make it. You do have an opinion, but you have little or no time to think of how to phrase it. You have too much respect for your friends (the audience) to waste their time or risk boring them with preliminaries.

1. You state your opinion briefly and rather bluntly. Suddenly Patricia is studying her fingernails. Bob is watching Patricia, seemingly more interested in her reaction than in the opinion itself. You can't tell exactly how either of them is reacting, though you know that if they agreed with you they would at least be looking at you. During this same fraction of a second, you glance at Alex and Suzy. Alex is frowning, and Suzy's eyebrows are raised.

2. If you were a shy person, you would be discouraged now and perhaps stop talking. But you aren't, and you believe strongly in your opinion, and you want your audience to share it. Realizing that a mere statement of it has not been enough to make them share it, you assume they have not understood. You fear you were too blunt, or perhaps a little vague. You want them to understand clearly what you meant, so you particularize the statement, adding detail. Patricia looks puz-

1

zled, but at least you're sure you have her attention. Now everyone is looking at you again. The other three faces register polite skepticism.

3. You make a statement to back and support your opinion. Bob puts down his cup and leans forward, watching you intently. The three others seem merely interested.

4. You give an illustration to anchor the supporting statement to familiar ground. Suzy smiles in recognition. You see signs of understanding in the others.

5. You make another supporting statement, this one simple enough to go unillustrated but not so immediately relevant to the opinion. Bob murmurs that he doesn't see the connection, and in two more sentences you make that relationship clear. He seems satisfied, and the others show signs of understanding, though not of agreement.

6. Watching now for signs (visual signals) that your friends are becoming convinced, you compare your opinion with a widely accepted opinion that it seems to resemble in important ways. Then you contrast it with one that it opposes, and you give reasons for the difference.

Then Patricia asks a question, and, before you can answer it, Alex rephrases it and adds a request for an example. You comply. Bob raises an objection. You counter. The interchange —the conversation—has resumed.[1]

Your "speech," which started as a mere statement of opinion and developed into an extempore presentation of a reasoned judgment, is now over. As your friends become speakers as well as listeners, the signals you receive are chiefly verbal. The visual signals, however, are still being sent and received.

Most oral communication is guided though not necessarily controlled by the facial and bodily movements (signals) of listeners (receivers). This silent guidance supplements oral

[1] As speaker in the six stages above, you did quite naturally what you might have done had you developed the same subject in an essay. You used specific principles of development, though probably without realizing that you were doing anything other than responding to circumstances, speaking as naturally as anyone else would in a like situation. (1) You stated a thesis (your opinion); (2) you backed it with particularizing details; (3, 4, 5) you supported it with two statements, illustrating one and explaining the relevance of the other; (6) you compared it and contrasted it with other opinions. Your oral presentation could serve as a framework for an essay.

signals of agreement or disagreement, understanding or lack of it. Such oral signs are often not complete sentences or even complete words, but they let the speaker (sender) know whether he is commmunicating.

As you were talking, you automatically watched your audience for signals that told you the degree of their understanding. You automatically obeyed these signals, whether they were conveyed by foreheads, eyebrows, lips, hands, or even feet. As soon as you saw recognition signals, you stopped working on one point and went on to another, one which you felt should logically follow.

However, if you had a tape recorder turned on while you were talking to the group and were to play it back immediately, you might be amazed to find that on a number of points you had not said nearly so much as you thought you had. You would notice also that some of your sentences were cut off and incomplete.

Your audience gave you the signal, and you responded by doing what you long ago learned to do—you went on to the next idea because there was no need to complete the sentence you knew your friends had already completed mentally. You were satisfied to provide the stimulus that called up in their minds the completion of your own thought. And so you talked in a kind of shorthand.

Most people depend upon the signals of recognition far more than they realize.

### Auxiliary Experiments

#### I

To convince yourself of the effect of listener signals on your speech, make a recording of yourself speaking impromptu on any subject. To be quite scientific, to concentrate most fully, or to deepen the psychological effect of aloneness, darken the room or take the tape recorder into a dark closet. Darkness is imperative, as is silence of course, if you conduct this experiment in a group. You must be utterly unable to receive listener-participation signals.

Immediately you are in a different element. You strain to be clear; you falter; you skip detail because it seems unnecessary, or you use more detail than you would ordinarily because your words sound so vulnerable, floating in the dark. You struggle to bring every sentence to completion—and so become more nearly precise.

Do you find yourself expending much more effort than you do when your friends are flashing signals of recognition? In the dark room with the tape recorder, you are very close to the situation you are in when you seat yourself before the typewriter and the blank sheet of paper.

## II

1. Almost any television program except a newscast will give you further proof. Simply close your eyes during the introductory commercial. Keep them closed as the program begins and for as long as you care to. Ten minutes should confuse entirely your concept of what is happening. If you close your eyes only after the program has begun, you will retain mental images of the actors and scenery, and confusion will take a bit longer. If you listen to a program that you watch regularly, you will, of course, already be familiar with many elements of it. Perhaps you can recognize the actors' voices without seeing their images on the screen, but even so you will realize much more fully than you did how very distinct the voices are one from another and how great a range of expression each single voice has.

2. You can conduct a slightly more elaborate experiment with the help of a friend. Tune in a television drama, and then keep your eyes closed from the beginning while the friend watches and listens to the program as he normally would. During a commercial or a station break, summarize your version of the plot so far. He will tell you how much you have missed and misunderstood.

## III

During almost any conversation, if you close your eyes and listen to the others speak, you will realize immediately how facial and bodily movements add to meaning. The words and sentences will seem disembodied and disconnected, much less cogent and probably much less important than they seemed when your eyes were open. Perhaps they won't seem very intelligent or even sensible.

## RESPONDING TO VOCAL SIGNALS

"But," you argue, "what makes you so sure that I depend on these signals you say I'm watching for? I don't have any trouble talking with my friends on the telephone, and I can't see them then, to watch their faces."

Words themselves are of course signals of a high order. But words carry additional signals in the way they're spoken—by variations in speed, inflection, voice level, pitch, tone; even by the calculated pauses between words. Even the most monotonous voice is loaded with interior communication. The voice can go so far as to reverse the meaning of words, as when you say ironically, "Wonderful weather!" on a dreary, wet day.

Because friends are so familiar with one another's speech, the slightest change in tone takes on meaning for them. Lovers who talk for hours on the telephone can forgo words completely for several minutes at a time; they have a method of conveying important messages by merely breathing at each other over the wires. These signals, primitive, emotional, closely akin to hand and finger touching, cannot communicate to strangers. They are not translatable. In writing, many words, carefully chosen, can only attempt to reproduce the effect of a certain smile, a grimace, an ironic shrug, a sarcastic undertone, a special, familiar sigh.

## *Auxiliary Experiment*

If you think that audience signals are not passed back and forth over the telephone, try taping a telephone conversation between friends who are discussing something of high interest to both. Even if one of them seems to be dominating the conversation, you will be amazed at the number of signals from the seemingly silent listener—the little *Hmms*, *Ohs*, *Ahs*, and *Mmms*. Then play the tape again, and this time listen carefully to the fluctuations in voice level and tone.

## Shifting from Talking to Writing

Visual or auditory signals are remarkable aids to conversation. They are a vital part of oral communication: they make it lively; they strip it of unnecessary words, parts of sentences, even whole sentences that would be needed to make writing clear but in friendly conversation are useless impedimenta. Conversation among friends is a living thing, vital, electric in its ability to convey even complicated thoughts. In it you can make the ellipsis, the gap over which you leap ahead, because friends are highly compatible senders and receivers. Like lovers, they have developed a sort of shorthand communication in their special signals. Fortunately, everybody learns to send and receive signals early in life and to depend on them.

Unfortunately, because of this dependence you may feel truly in the dark when you try to communicate through the written rather than the spoken word.

If you do, you are not alone, even among college students. Among them are many excellent speakers, many whose oral communication is lucid and fluent. For them as for most people, talking is easier than writing. You yourself may have wondered more than once, "Why is it that I don't have any trouble talking to almost anybody, and yet the minute I try to write an essay, I have nothing to say and no way of saying it?"

In the first stages of writing, the inhibiting agent is the lack of signals the writer is accustomed, as a speaker, to receiving from his listener. These signals tell him when to go on, when to add more detail, when to give an illustration, to make a comparison or a contrast, to begin a new development, to define his terms, or to stop and recapitulate. Obedience to the signals is automatic. The sender is never required to make an evaluation of his own efforts; his audience makes the evaluation for him. Similarly, the impromptu speaker may or may not be aware of the process of development he is using. In a writing situation, therefore, he may not realize the necessity of a thought-through method of development.

And his reader, from whom not the faintest signal comes, seems indeed remote.

## NO, YOU CAN'T WRITE AS YOU TALK

There are those who maintain that all your writing troubles will be over if you only "write as you talk." You'd have more trouble than ever if you followed this advice literally.

The processes of writing and of talking are not the same, and to confuse the two is naïve.

Talking and writing are two separate modes of communication, and, though they have much in common, they are fundamentally different. Just as you long ago learned to use one set of signals when you talk, you must learn to use another set of signals for your writing.

There are those who seem to follow successfully the "write as you talk" theory (not, however, as it is usually interpreted or even usually intended). Most successful among these are the business correspondents who answer scores of letters daily. The writing of many of these correspondents is amazingly complete and accurate, yet concise. But they do not work without planning their letters or anticipating their readers' reactions.

In answering letters, the correspondent uses simple guides which, in effect, seat his reader before him. Through a letter, the reader has asked for specific information or requested the answers to specific questions. The correspondent reads the letter carefully, makes marginal notes, and dictates an answer. He has an almost perfect organizational guide in the letter he is answering. Furthermore, he has studied his subject —a product or service—carefully, knows it thoroughly, has a fund of information which he has already phrased in expository terms, and has already formulated his answers before he begins dictation. He is usually an expert in the psychology of tone: he can read between the lines in the letters he must answer, and he can control the tone and therefore the psychological effect of the letters he writes. After long experience, he can convey a conversational touch in the most mundane correspondence—if in his judgment it is appropriate.

Yet he cannot truly be said to "write as he talks." When he

turns in his chair to talk to his secretary or to a fellow worker, he reverts immediately and automatically to the set of signals he has learned in his conversational experience, which extends to his childhood.

## YOUR READER DOESN'T KNOW YOU

The column on the left below records the kind of talk with which everyone is familiar. The column on the right indicates what a writer must do to fill in the huge gaps in meaning that talkers with compatible experience backgrounds hurdle effortlessly.

### Conversation Between Jim and Steve

| *The Words Used* | *The Message Actually Conveyed* |
|---|---|
| "Hi, Jim."<br>"Hi, Steve." | The tone of the speakers' voices indicates familiarity, shared experience, and community of interest. The animation of their greeting suggests a high interest in each other as well as an anticipation of interesting news to be shared. |
| "Hey, you know that MG of Bill's?" | The identification of Bill's MG is complete. Both speakers have ridden in it, driven it, helped Bill work on it; they are completely familiar with all its eccentricities. The very mention of it brings to Jim's mind scores, perhaps hundreds of recollections. He does not have to have the MG identified by year, model, horsepower, size, weight, speed, color, or condition. |
| "Yeah?" | Jim's reply is prompted, not by any necessity of communication, but merely by a desire to get into the game, to share an experience at a more intense |

level than can be indicated by silence.

Because of the experience that Jim and Steve shared the week before, the question need not be asked. The words "fuel pump" would be enough to replay in Jim's mind the work of the previous Saturday afternoon. He remembers the broken fuel pump, the telephone calls to every automobile-parts store in town, the blank feeling that came upon the boys when they finally realized that there was not a single new fuel pump in town that would fit the MG. He remembers their calls to automobile junk yards, the triumphant feeling when they finally located a wrecked MG that still had on the engine a fuel pump with possibly a few hours of service left. Jim's recognition of the common concern flashes to Steve in a single look.

"Remember the fuel pump?"

"You don't mean?"

Common to both boys is the knowledge that the used fuel pump could last two minutes, two hours, or two years.

"Right."

Jim now knows that the used fuel pump has failed.

"When?"
"Coming home from the lake last night."

Jim knows the road, a back road with only a few farmhouses scattered along the thirty miles. He does not have to be told of the long walk home.

Steve and Jim communicated. In only 28 words they conveyed to each other meanings that 325 words in the opposite column can only summarize. The 28-word dialogue by itself, though it is now in the *form* of writing, cannot be called clear writing. Without the explanation in the right-hand column, it is little more than a stark, incoherent series of words to anyone other than Steve and Jim. The details that pack the exchange with meaning to the two close friends are not explicit in the words of the dialogue.

For the sake of brevity and out of common sense, speakers take into account what they know their listeners are already aware of. Jim would have gone mad from impatience if Steve had repeated all the information in the right-hand column above.

## *Auxiliary Experiments*

### I

Conduct your own Steve-Jim experiment as a field project in constructive eavesdropping. Station yourself with pad and pencil at a place where and a time when you can unobtrusively overhear those who are strangers to you but friends of each other meet, converse briefly, and go on their ways. The head or the foot of a wide stairway in almost any campus building can be a good eavesdropping station between classes. A snack bar or bookstore on or near campus is good during its busy times.

1.  Simply jot down exactly what they say. You may, but you need not, note tone, gestures, and facial expressions if these signals substitute for speech. It is best to record entire conversations. But if it is not possible—if your subjects talk on and on, or if they leave or you must leave—at least record in its entirety a part of a longer conversation which is devoted to a particular subject. Even though you do not know what the subject is, you will quite naturally be aware when it is dropped and another taken up.

2.  You have now recorded three or four short conversations, in whole or part. Allow at least an hour to elapse. Then choose the most enigmatic, and translate each speech in it, as the Steve-Jim conversation was translated, to make it intelligible to a stranger—to yourself, in this case. How accurate you are you will probably never know.

It is quite probable that from one conversation you can derive several meanings. Here, as an example, is the opening fragment of a perfectly ordinary college-stairway conversation, with a few ideas for possible interpretations:

| *Conversation* | *Possible Meanings* |
| --- | --- |
| Girl X: Hi! | |
| Girl Y: (Long groan, followed by a sigh, both accompanied by an eloquent sagging of the body, a near stagger) | Despair?<br>Remembered anguish? |
| Girl X:   That bad, was it? | Since the girls last saw each other, Y has had an experience that both knew she would have. That experience is the implied antecedent of the pronoun *it*:<br>1.   Examination?<br>2.   Zoology experiment?<br>3.   Blind date?<br>4.   Dentist's appointment?<br>5.   Y's breaking of her engagement? |
| Girl Y:   He was ghastly! Awful! | 1.   The professor?<br>2.   Her laboratory partner?<br>      The dead cat she dissected?<br>3.   Her escort?<br>4.   The dentist?<br>5.   Her fiancé? |

3. In a paragraph or two, expand one of your interpretations. Describe the event your conversationalists may have been discussing. Attach a copy of the conversation you overheard.

## II

A sporting event separately televised and radio-broadcast offers the basis for another experiment. Team sports such as baseball or football are ideal. (A horse race would probably be least satisfactory because of its brevity.)

Tune in a game on both television and radio. Then turn down the volume on television, and watch the screen as you listen to the radio account. Before half an hour has passed, you will have experienced either or both of the following: You do not watch the screen nearly so closely as you do normally, simply because it is unnecessary. Or you are amused or annoyed with the obviousness of the radio commentary: much of it is superfluous to someone who is watching the game.

Then turn the radio off. Turn up the volume on the television set, and turn the brightness control until the screen is black. You will find yourself straining to follow the progress of the game, because the announcer assumes you can see it, just as the radio announcer assumes you can't.

The radio announcer's job is more nearly that of the writer than is the television announcer's. Yet he gives more than words to his audience. His voice is full of signals.

## Writer and Reader

The spoken word and the written word are two separate media, both springing from the same wish to communicate and both subject to organization and development. Yet one depends on personal rapport or on a subconsciously mastered set of signals, whereas the other demands a rigorous analysis of audience background and a fine selection and elimination of details.

But how can you do a rigorous analysis of the background of an audience you can't see? How do you even know who the reading audience is?

### THE READER AS INESCAPABLE

For whom should you write—your friends, your instructor, your classmates, an imaginary group of people you'd like to impress? Should you perhaps write for yourself and let the chips fall where they may?

It is of course vital to consider yourself in your writing: you can hardly hope to interest anyone else in something that has not interested you. But writing implies a reader. To give the excuse that you want to write for yourself and are not interested in reader reaction is to avoid the main purpose of writing—communication.

Other purposes there are, the keeping of journals and diaries in which writers can reveal their inmost thoughts and store them for later. The journal or diary can be a psychiatric couch or a confessional. (It can provide a personal history for one's descendants, but then of course it is communicating.) It is best of all a means of practicing expression and gaining fluency.[2] Of first-rate journals and diaries not originally intended for publication, literature knows but few, and those that have been brought forth—usually heavily edited by strangers long after the death of the authors—generally impress readers more by the striking power of individual lines and paragraphs than by their engagement with life. The desk drawer is not the marketplace where ideas are brought out to be modified, adopted, or abandoned.

If you do write for yourself, when you share what you've written, you must be prepared to be misunderstood. (For example, it is rare that one student's class notes can be useful to another student.) Perhaps you remember how far the argument "But it's clear to *me!*" took you with your high-school English teacher who marked a part of your writing with a question mark or labeled it with "Unclear" or "Explain."

You will be sharing your writing, and you might as well intend it as communication. Your writing will be read, not only in this course but in others throughout your career in college. To a large extent, fair or not, you will be judged through your writing, not only in college but out of it, now and throughout your life, whether you are writing an essay for your class, a letter of application,[3] a report for your employer, a

---

[2] See page 124 for a further discussion of the journal.

[3] The following letter is an application for admission to the executive training program of a large department store. Although the company was then actively recruiting graduating college seniors as trainees, the personnel director gave the letter to his secretary with this notation: "Margaret, please tell him we can't consider him at this time."

Dear Mr. XX:

    I am desirous of securing placement in a Trainee program. I expect to graduate from YY University January 29. I expect to receive a Bachelor of Science in Business Administration.

    I am attaching a copy of my résumé for your review and con-

speech before Congress, or a note to the milkman.

It takes two—at least—to communicate. Think of the sender and the receiver. A speaker must have an audience; a writer must have a reader, and he must write for that reader if what he writes is to be understood.

## THE FRIEND AS READER

If you write for your friend, you will be in constant danger of writing as you would talk to him (remember Steve and Jim?), of relying on what you know he knows and thereby being less than intelligible to anyone else. True enough, the better the reader knows you, the greater chance your writing has of being understood; it will be received with sympathy if you are liked by the reader, with joy if you are loved.

## THE INSTRUCTOR AS READER

*Can you make him sympathetic?* Isn't it really the instructor you have to worry about now? So that's why his office is crowded with students! They want him to know them and thus to look sympathetically upon their work. Is life then so simple?

No. There is a sacred literary commandment to judge the author by his works and not the works by their author. Even if there were not, that office is already crowded, the hours are all booked: too many students, too few office hours.

*Can you analyze his preferences?* Does "rigorous analysis of the background of an audience" mean research the instructor? Can you find out what he likes and write about that? You don't have time.

Besides, if researching instructors in English worked, researching those in your other courses would, too. You'd spend all your time lurking about the offices. (Some students do, of course.) When you research instructors, the job is endless: each term start all over, prowl new corridors. Fur-

---

sideration. I would appreciate an application. Any correspondence addressed to my home address would receive my prompt attention.

Yours truly,

ZZ

thermore, suppose you have learned your history instructor is fond of motorcycles. How do you work them into your essay answers in an examination on the French Revolution?

*Can you tell him something new?* Can you assume the instructor likes to learn as well as teach? In your essays you can teach him what you know about dune buggies, or harpsichords, or the batting records of American League third basemen—unless he already knows about these. If so, how much does he know? Did he hear a harpsichord once and like the sound of it, or does he play one? You still have to find out at which level to work.

You may have noticed that *what* to write about becomes a problem when you are concerned primarily with *pleasing* the reader. *The reader's understanding is the effect you write for; his pleasure will come as a side effect.*

It is true that faculty or their assistants will be reading your writing as long as you are in college. Yet, though subject matter for student writing is imposed and circumscribed far more in other courses than in English composition, in neither is your writing read primarily to learn about the subject of it. If your history instructor wants to learn more about history than he presently knows, he goes to a history book, to another historian, rather than to your examination booklet or term paper. In the essay examination or the term paper he discovers what you have learned: not simply how much but how well. He learns whether you know the material and, more important, how thoughtfully you deal with it. He looks not simply for facts but for relationships among them; not simply for data but for your analysis of them, or your synthesis of them into some meaningful pattern; not merely for information but for your development of it in some progression toward a point.

The question in the essay examination provides a focus on the point or points your answer should make. In English composition the subject and the method of its development may be prescribed or not for a particular essay, but your thesis [4] will focus the essay upon a point as the question does in an examination. Actually, in English composition, you write the

[4] The thesis as such will be examined in Chapter Two.

question *and* its answer, not merely the latter.

English composition does not have its own limited body of subject matter on which you write, as do other courses. Here more than in the others it is not so much the subject of your essay as what you do with it, how you handle it, for these two are the primary concern of this course. Instructors in other courses would like to assume that your writing is an accurate reflection of your thinking about a body of knowledge. The composition instructor is concerned with your thinking out into writing.

*Should you write up to him?* Should you then write *up* to the instructor of English, history, or whatever? The first is only indirectly concerned with subject, the others prescribe it, and they all judge you as student by your treatment of it.

If you write "up," your writing will be stilted. (Hence the expression, of course—think of putting your ideas and words on stilts.) You will be trying to convey the impression that your knowledge of the subject is more thorough than it is or that the subject is more important than you know it to be. Somehow, from the pseudo heights of stilted expression you will try to convey the idea that you have reached profound depths of understanding. You will appear more ludicrous than learned. The subject will betray you because you will set yourself a grandiose thesis, one which you can only fake, not develop. Your vocabulary will betray you. And your sentences, which should move tightly forward, will falter and wander off, deserting your thesis. The result will be bathos, the silly disaster an amateur hypocrite deserves. You will be understood only too well.

*Should you write down to him?* To make yourself perfectly clear, then, should you write *down*, that is, for someone less intelligent or less sophisticated than you? No, for three reasons. First of all, without great effort you'll not respect such a reader, and your writing will reflect condescension, which is insulting. Second, in straining to simplify your treatment of a subject, you may oversimplify the subject too, or distort it, thereby falsifying it.[5] Third, the instructor, not

[5] Simplicity and clarity, incidentally, are quite separate concepts. The two terms are not interchangeable, though many people use them as if they were.

Simple Simon, will be reading the essay, and how can you at the same time write for the latter and let the former know that you know more than the essay pretends you do?

*What is his role?* Think of the instructor who will judge your essays as a comfortable, unobtrusive observer of a communication between two others, one of whom (the sender) is you, the writer, and the other (the silent receiver) is a hypothetical reader.

## THE HYPOTHETICAL READER

*Who is he?* If you are not to write up or down, if you are to make what you have to say clear to someone who does not yet know about it or believe in it or agree with it, you'll need a reader much like you and yet different from you in important ways. This reader should be as intelligent as you; his general background, including education, should be equal to yours; he should be as sophisticated and as sensitive as you. He should be a bit difficult to convince or sway. *And he should have no* SPECIAL *knowledge of the subject your essay treats.* If you write about cats, he has no previous special understanding of cats but does understand dogs. If you write about dogs, he has no previous special understanding of dogs, though he understands cats. You, the writer, are the specialist, the expert. Your reader must be the intelligent layman whom you will try to enlighten or convince or persuade.

For any particular essay, this hypothetical reader—rather like you but without your specialized knowledge of the subject you are treating—may well be a real person too, one of your classmates perhaps. But looking for that real person is chancy and time-consuming. Furthermore, unless you were to write on the same subject all term, you'd have to find a new reader for each essay. If you lumped these real readers, if you wrote all your essays for all your classmates, you'd find yourself in difficulty because they vary widely in their interests and specialized knowledge. Being all things to all men, as you would have to be, is a difficult accomplishment indeed. If it weren't, Cleopatra would have been forgotten long ago. And politics would be a basic science, not an art.

So write for your hypothetical reader. You'll not waste time trying to find him, trying to investigate him, trying to outguess him, trying to flatter him. For him you'll be able to write with honesty and clarity and precision on any subject you know. Writing will be easier for you. And paradoxically, if you write for him, you will be able to communicate much more to many more real readers than you can any other way. Your English instructor will see what you have written rather than the smoke screen covering it; he will see you rather than see through you. In any other course for which you write, your writing will be more meaningful, and that instructor will be able to see how much you have learned, not how little you have managed to communicate.

If your writing is expository, your all-purpose, adjustable hypothetical reader happens not to know whatever it is you are explaining, though he has a general preparation for understanding it.[6] If your writing is descriptive, he has never before seen what you describe, or he has seen it but not as you have. If your writing is argumentative, he is one who tends toward the view opposed to the one you are arguing. If your writing is persuasive, he would be unpersuaded were it not for you. For example, if your thesis or proposition is on behalf of the Republican party, your reader is a Democrat. Two enthusiastic Republicans communicating to each other their enthusiasm for the Republican party can make themselves clear with as few details as Steve and Jim needed when they discussed the MG. If your thesis is in praise of a candidate for Republican nomination, however, your reader can be Republican, but he must not be a supporter of your candidate. If

[6] For most writing in almost any course other than composition, you assume that the hypothetical reader has fulfilled the requirements for entrance into the course. In an upper-level course, he has taken the prerequisite courses. You do not assume that he has completed the course for which you are writing; either he has not taken it at all, or he is a unit or chapter or quiz period behind you, the writer. For example, if you are writing an essay examination in a course in the history of the American Civil War, your reader has a broad knowledge of American history and a respectable memory (you should not waste time identifying Abraham Lincoln for him), but he has not studied this period of American history in depth. If you prepare a research paper on a special topic for the course, you can assume your reader is taking the course but has not gone deeply into this aspect of it. It is you who take him further into it, and you who must see that he does not lose his way.

you want to persuade someone to join the Peace Corps, don't waste time on someone who is already in it.

*How do you use him?* For this hypothetical reader your writing will be far stronger than it is likely to be otherwise. You will be able to edit it with greater objectivity. Simply switch roles, temporarily assuming that of the hypothetical reader. You will be alert to the need for filling gaps you might otherwise not have noticed. You will give yourself signals as if a real reader were sitting before you and sending them.

As you think through anything you are going to write, take advantage of the questions you know your hypothetical reader will ask. Why not ask similar questions of yourself before you write?

Am I worrying too much about pleasing him, instead of trying to be clear?

Am I writing down to him?

Am I repeating things that are obvious to both of us?

Am I swaying him to my ideas, or am I merely presenting my ideas?

The inadequacies in the following essay would be less glaring if the writer had considered the hypothetical reader. Questions and comments from the latter are in the second column.

### The Best Car for a Young Person

I want to write about something that interests young people more than anything else does, namely a car. Young people want cars because they are necessary for school, work, and recreation. The most popular car for young people is a car that has a stick shift instead of an automatic shift. A shift has to be operated by hand, and the driver must also operate a clutch with

If you want to write, get started.

You aren't telling me anything I didn't know. That's why everybody wants a car.

Don't you know that there's also a column shift?
I know how to drive both automatic and shift cars. You're wasting my time.

his foot before he shifts. Learning to drive a shift car is harder than learning to drive a car with an automatic shift. It requires a knowledge of when to shift and how to shift without grinding the gears and even stripping them so that they must be repaired.

> I could have assumed this from your last sentence, which wasn't news to me either.

Some shift-car drivers brag about how they can beat an automatic-shift car at the traffic light every time because they can rev up before they let out the clutch. This, however, is dangerous because they might not take time to see whether there is someone from the right or the left trying to run the "pink" light at the last moment.

> Are you talking about cars or about stick shifts? Take another look at your title.

> I've heard shift cars rev up a few times myself.

I think that all these considerations should enter into the buying of a car. Older people might think that young people want a shift car in order to show off, but that is not so. What they want is something they can think about as they shift from one gear to another. The automatic shift makes the driver start daydreaming because he has nothing to think about. It is the unthinking driver that causes accidents. Young people are also better able to handle shift cars because their reactions are faster. So there is no doubt about the shift car being the best car for a young person.

> My mother told me that the first day of kindergarten.

> What considerations?

> Do you mean that the activity of shifting helps them concentrate on their driving?

> He still has a steering wheel and a speedometer, for instance.

> Better than who?
> Faster than what?
> I'm glad you're convinced.
> I'm not.

Here is the beginning of a better essay, one whose writer kept the hypothetical reader in mind.

### The Stick-Shift People

Managers of used-car lots know more about customer likes and dislikes than the customers do themselves. When a new-car dealer takes in a clean three-year-old Chevrolet, Ford, or Plymouth with under ten thousand miles on the speedometer, almost flawless upholstery, and no rust spots or dents, his used-car manager takes one quick look at the front compartment. Then he shrugs his shoulders, or points to the back of the lot, or smiles happily.

If he shrugs, the trade-in has an automatic shift. If he points to the back of the lot, it has a column shift. If he smiles, it has a stick shift. The automatic will stay on the back of the lot until a middle-aged couple that wants a nice car but can't afford a new one happens along. The column-shift trade-in will stay on the back of the lot until some avid penny pincher, strong on saving gasoline but absolutely devoid of soul, walks to the back of the lot looking for *exactly* that kind of car. But the stick shift is another matter. The manager knows at least five young people who will be on the lot fifteen minutes after he calls them. He knows he can not only sell this car fast but charge extra.

Why?

The automatic is only good transportation. The column-shift car is good transportation with built-in extra mileage and almost guaranteed savings. But the stick-shift, with the deep growl of its first gear, the lovely whine of the second, is far more than mere transportation. It is excitement. It is competition. It is challenge. It is an ego builder. It is a chance for. . . .

Notice the movement and action in the beginning paragraph. The writer here employs the used-car manager to support his own views, thereby eliminating the use of the unsupported *I* and cutting off the hypothetical reader before he asks, "Who are *you* to be telling *me*, Bud?" By describing those customers who prefer the automatic- and the column-shift cars, the writer sets up a sharp contrast for later development. The division of automobiles as automatic-, column-, and stick-shift, repeated to accentuate the differences in purchasers, is a sophisticated means of development that will satisfy the sensitive hypothetical reader. Without being explicitly told, the reader realizes that the writer is rifling in on the kind of person who thrives on excitement and challenge. The composition that seems at first to be about cars will reveal much about people—a far more interesting subject.

The hypothetical reader can also help the writer keep from losing his cool. Those who have strong feelings on a subject sometimes become preoccupied, when they write, with letting it be known that they have these feelings rather than communicating them in such a way that a reader can share them. The resulting outburst may be silly, or foolish, or lugubrious, or hysterical. It reveals little save that the writer *has* such-and-such an opinion. It explains little, if anything. If the reader forms a new opinion from it, it is that the writer is dull, or silly, or foolish.

## Auxiliary Experiments

### I

The following essays seem to be attempts to let off steam rather than to communicate or convince. Comment on each as the hypothetical reader does in the example on pages 19-20. Discuss how in each case the writer could have improved his presentation if he had considered the hypothetical reader. Whether you agree or disagree with the opinion, do not praise or censure it as such; rather, comment on the backing the writer gives it or might have given it.

1.                    A Ridiculous Proposal

I think the proposal by our city personnel director that a human-relations council be established is ridiculous.

In the first place, it is totally unnecessary. It seems to me that he just wants to spend our tax money to create a position in our city government that is totally unnecessary. As far as I know, we have practically no minority groups living in our city, and it will probably be a long time before this situation changes.

The personnel director's proposal appears to be "crossing a bridge before we come to it." I know there is a certain amount of political prestige involved in promoting open housing, human-relations councils, etc. However, as far as I am concerned, all the emphasis in this area is so much political vote getting and succumbing to pressure groups.

Since the day this country was founded, as far as I know, any citizen, whether red, white, blue, or any other color, has had a legal right to buy a house or do anything any other citizen could do. I stress the word "legal" because this should be the only element of consideration. We all know that economically, in the free-enterprise system, people are not equal, and let's hope this never changes. If it does, we will be living under total Socialism, a growing trend in this country since 1932 which has got to distress any real American.

2.                    Let's Get Something for Our Taxes

In regard to trash collection, it would seem to me that with the advent of the city income tax on top of all our other taxes the city should at least provide city garbage collection for the taxpayers.

I don't know whether or not garbage collection by the city is more efficient or less efficient than having it done by private contractors, but I do feel that if we citizens have to pay such high taxes as we do then we should get a few minimum city services, such as garbage collection by the city. If the city feels it doesn't want to provide certain of these minimum services, then the city income tax should be abolished.

3.                    The Role of the Modern University

Education must be active, not passive. The day of traditional, structured, lock-step education is past, long past. This university is a relic of the Dark Ages: its curriculum is medieval, its faculty is monkish, its administration inquisitorial.

The students at this unversity must show their muscle. They must arise and be no longer sheep in a flock, shepherded by the pious automatons that call themselves faculty. We must seize upon every tactic and strategy—and muscle—and throw off the shackles under which we groan. We must unleash that force that has been sleeping in acquiescence to the "father-knows-best" attitude of this administration. We must shake off our stupor. We must have change!

We must, we will, bring changes in all areas of university

life. We will make this university viable and relevant to the real world. If necessary, we must be prepared to drag this Victorian administration kicking and screaming into this period of change.

The faculty will be our biggest stumbling block, but they can be led if we show them innovations and experiments. We are not trying to be dictatorial. There *can* be education without classes being a structured string of lectures which must be regurgitated verbatim in examinations. We need and we must insist on a change in attitude on the part of the faculty in all facets of the university. They have not been allowed to follow their own goals. They don't know what the goal of education is. They are afraid of the innovative. They are apathetic; they are afraid of involvement with the community, where the university must serve a larger purpose, where we can solve the problems of the ghetto, of police brutality, of the oppressive hand of city hall.

We must keep stressing the continuing function of the modern university in the world today.

## II

Read the letters-to-the-editor section of the campus newspaper or any other newspaper. Find at least one letter which would have benefited if the writer had used the device of the hypothetical reader. As you did in the examples above, comment on the treatment of the subject, as it is and as it might have been. Remember to grant the writer his opinion. Discuss only his support and defense of it.

### FRIENDS AS CRITICS

Your classmates, friends, and acquaintances—even your enemies—are good sounding boards for what you have to say. You can test on them the clarity and effectiveness of your writing. Ask them to be your critics.

Of course, your instructor may devote class time to the analysis and criticism of student papers. He may project some of them on a screen, or he may duplicate them and distribute copies. He may have you exchange essays and write your comments and criticism.

But even if he does all or none of these, you should if possible exchange papers with other students outside the class-room. You can discuss, analyze, and criticize one another's papers informally, and you can learn much. From your colleagues' handling of problems you can better understand your own. From their comments on your own paper, you can learn your strengths and weaknesses. Remember, however, that if you write about your automobile, someone who recently helped you repair it should not be the sole judge of that essay.

Of course, you must insist on frankness if you ask a colleague to read your paper, and you must be prepared to receive it, whether or not you accept its validity. The frank criticism of a friend can be harsher than that of an instructor. Whereas the latter tends to confine his reactions to polite notations such as "Unclear," your roommate may snort at you, "This part doesn't make any sense." The next step is to find out exactly what and why and how, not to take affront. If you are hypersensitive about your writing, if you take criticism of it personally rather than objectively, you cannot profit from sharing it with anyone. You might as well forget the reader and write for yourself alone. You might as well not write at all.

CHAPTER TWO

# Subject and Thesis

## Man and Universals in Good Writing

But after a while, I was glad I had seen the cars in this
natural setting, which was, after all, a kind of Plato's Republic
for teen-agers. Because if you watched anything at this fair
very long, you kept noticing the same thing. These kids are
absolutely maniacal about form. They are practically religious
about it. For example, the dancers: none of them ever smiled.
They stared at each other's legs and feet, concentrating. The
dances had no grace about them at all, they were more in the
nature of a hoedown, but everybody was concentrating to do
them exactly *right*. And the bouffant kids all had form, wild
form, but form with rigid standards, one gathers. Even the
boys. Their dress was prosaic—Levis, Slim Jims, sport shirts,
T shirts, polo shirts—but the form was consistent: a stove-
pipe silhouette. And they all had the same hairstyle: some
wore it long, some short, but none of them had a part; all
that hair was brushed back straight from the hairline. I went
by one of the guitar booths, and there was a little kid in there,
about thirteen, playing the hell out of an electric guitar. The
kid was named Cranston something or other. He looked liked
he ought to be named Kermet or Herschel; all his genes were
kind of horribly Okie. Cranston was playing away and a big
crowd was watching. But Cranston was slouched back with his
spine bent like a sapling up against a table, looking gloriously
bored. At thirteen, this kid was being fanatically cool. They
all were. They were all wonderful slaves to form. They have
created their own style of life, and they are much more
authoritarian about enforcing it than are adults. Not only

that, but today these kids—especially in California—have *money*, which needless to say, is why all these shoe merchants and guitar sellers and the Ford Motor Company were at a Teen Fair in the first place. I don't mind observing that it is this same combination—money plus slavish devotion to form—that accounts for Versailles or St. Mark's square. Naturally, most of the artifacts that these kids' money-plus-form produce are of a pretty ghastly order. But so was most of the paraphernalia that developed in England during the Regency. I mean, most of it was on the order of starched cravats. A man could walk into Beau Brummel's house at 11 A.M., and here would come the butler with a tray of wilted linen. "These were some of our failures," he confides. But then Brummel comes downstairs wearing one perfect starched cravat. Like one perfect iris, the flower of Mayfair civilization. But the Regency period did see some tremendous formal architecture. And the kids' formal society has also brought at least one substantial thing to a formal development of a high order—the customized cars. I don't have to dwell on the point that cars mean more to these kids than architecture did in Europe's great formal century, say, 1750 to 1850. They are freedom, style, sex, power, motion, color—everything is right there.[1]

This passage is an excerpt from Tom Wolfe's essay "The Kandy-Kolored, Tangerine-Flake, Streamline Baby," from which his book of essays takes its title. Although his title might lead you to expect customized cars to be his central concern in this work, Mr. Wolfe is interested in them primarily as a means of studying far more interesting subjects— the young Californians developing a new art form and a new style of living. The customized cars are symbols of these; they are merely evidence of profound changes in thinking among members of the privileged youth groups. He observes the teen-agers' concentration upon form in their dancing, their dress, their music, their demeanor, their conduct. He asserts that the teen-agers who have developed a new culture are "authoritative about enforcing it."

[1] Tom Wolfe, *The Kandy-Kolored, Tangerine-Flake, Streamline Baby* (New York: Farrar, Straus and Giroux, 1965), pp. 78-79. Copyright © 1965 by Tom Wolfe. Reprinted by permission of the publisher.

### INSIGHT REVEALS UNIVERSALS

His emphasis on the universal allegiance to conformity indicates that Mr. Wolfe went to California not to describe what he saw (although he does that with distinction) but to look until he got some insight into what was taking place there, until he was able to describe what he saw in terms of universal human needs. Mr. Wolfe *transformed* what he saw into a statement about human living under certain conditions.

### GOOD WRITING IMPLIES UNIVERSALS

Great writing, lasting writing, good writing, interesting writing—almost all worthwhile writing except some of the most highly technical concerns itself with universals. That is, it concerns itself with human qualities and experiences which are shared at least potentially by all mankind. Because it is thus relevant to his own human qualities and experiences—real, vicarious, potential—the reader can share in it. He can like it.

Universals are within the range of experience, real or vicarious, of everyone who has ever lived. They include fear, anger, love, pity, pride, sorrow, compassion, loneliness, sacrifice, honor, shame; the desire for understanding, for justification, for knowledge, for success, for survival, for existence after death, for peace. Such universals have directed men's energies for thousands of years. The power of universals is almost beyond belief; for them men have sacrificed their lives and the lives of others throughout history. Universals are constant; they renew themselves for each generation. For each generation, they are real, and they seem new. Each man discovers them as if he were Adam.

Whenever a universal is present in a piece of writing, the reader can reach out in recognition: "Yes, that's how it is" or "That's how it would be." The mind of the reader can become consubstantial with the mind of the writer. If the universals are there and the writing is good, the two minds are together, and the reader and the writer are brothers.

Henry David Thoreau, in *Walden,* writes about man and nature, the two practically inseparable. Even as he was exploring the animal and plant life around Walden Pond, he explored his own life and the life of man. His interest in nature, though avid, was secondary.

> I went to the woods because I wished to live deliberately, to front only the essential facts of life, and see if I could not learn what it had to teach, and not, when I came to die, discover that I had not lived. I did not wish to live what was not life, living is so dear; nor did I wish to practice resignation, unless it was quite necessary. I wanted to live deep and suck out all the marrow of life, to live so sturdily and Spartan-like as to put to rout all that was not life, to cut a broad swath and shave close, to drive life into a corner, and reduce it to its lowest terms, and, if it proved to be mean, why then to get the whole and genuine meanness of it, and publish its meanness to the world; or if it were sublime, to know it by experience, and be able to give a true account of it. . . .[2]

In this passage from *The Stones of Venice* (1850), the great English art critic John Ruskin admires Venetian glass, but beyond that admiration glows his love of the kind of society that produced the kind of men that produced that glass.

> Our modern glass is exquisitely clear in its substance, true in its form, accurate in its cutting. We are proud of this. We ought to be ashamed of it. The old Venice glass was muddy, inaccurate in all its forms, and clumsily cut, if at all. And the old Venetian was justly proud of it. For there is this difference between the English and Venetian workman, that the former thinks only of accurately matching his patterns, and getting his curves perfectly true and his edges perfectly sharp, and becomes a mere machine for rounding curves and sharpening edges, while the old Venetian cared not a whit whether his edges were sharp or not, but he invented a new design for every glass that he made, and never molded a handle or a lip without a new fancy in it. And therefore, though some Venetian glass is ugly and clumsy enough, when made by clumsy and uninventive workmen, other Venetian glass is so lovely in its forms that no price is too great for it; and we never see the same form in it twice. Now you cannot have the finish and the varied form too. If the workman is thinking about his edges, he cannot be thinking of his

[2] Henry David Thoreau, *Walden* (1854).

design; if of his design, he cannot think of his edges. Choose whether you will pay for the lovely form or the perfect finish, and choose at the same moment whether you will make the worker a man or a grindstone.[3]

Even Thomas Henry Huxley's "The Method of Scientific Investigation" has as its center man the thinker. To convince his nineteenth-century audience that the study of science contributes to the quality of life for anyone, scientist or not, and that it should be part of a liberal education, Huxley gave a series of lectures. In "The Method of Scientific Investigation," his classic "easy explanation" of how men of science proceed is so engaging that modern readers may not realize his primary concern is in the development of man the thinker. The following passage makes the universal connection in order to give reassurance that the scientific method, at least in its elementary stages, is little more than a guided and thoughtful doing of something man has always done unconsciously.

> There is a well-known incident in one of Molière's plays, where the author makes the hero express unbounded delight on being told that he had been talking prose during the whole of his life. In the same way, I trust that you will take comfort, and be delighted with yourselves, on the discovery that you have been acting on the principles of inductive and deductive philosophy during the same period. Probably there is no one here who has not in the course of the day had occasion to set in motion a complex train of reasoning, of the very same kind, though differing of course in degree, as that which a scientific man goes through in tracing the causes of natural phenomena.[4]

## UNIVERSALS LINK WRITERS AND READERS

Before you became aware of universals (in this book or elsewhere), if you had been asked why you liked such-and-such a work, you would probably have answered, "Because it is interesting" or "Because it is exciting" or "Because I felt as if I were taking part in the story." The reason behind each of

[3] John Ruskin, *The Stones of Venice* (1850).
[4] Thomas Henry Huxley, "The Method of Scientific Investigation."

these reasons is the presence of universals. The reasons are evidence of that presence. Great and even merely good literature is cogently universal; it has universality.

Sholom Aleichem wrote simple stories about poor, obscure Jewish people. The stories have humor and pathos; the hopes and cares of the characters are universal hopes and cares. Laid in Russia in the nineteenth century, written in Yiddish, translated into other languages, adapted into other art forms (for first the stage and then the screen), interpreted by directors, expressed by actors, translated into still other languages for dubbing-in, the stories are loved because their universals have endured and are recognized. When the movie *Fiddler on the Roof* (from *Tevye's Daughters*) opened in Japan, the Japanese asked in wonder, "Do they really understand this in America? This is very Japanese!" It is very *everybody*, though it is about only a few "little" people who lived in Russia a hundred years ago. Universals appeal across time, space, languages, and cultures.

Certainly literature can deal with universals and still fail, for any number of reasons; but if it succeeds—if it involves you in itself, if it makes itself memorable to the reader—it assuredly deals with universals. Without these, there is no valid link between the characters and their action, between the work and its author as a human being; no real connection between the reader and the work he reads, and therefore no lasting interest in it and little memory of it after he finishes it. The ultimate subject of a work of literature worth the reading is a universal one.

# Finding Subject-Man-Universal Relationships

## THE CENTER OF MAN'S CONCERN

In freshman composition, certainly, your concern is with universals as they are useful to you in writing assignments. Yet looking for universals will help you not only in your writing for this course and others, but in almost any writing you will ever do, in your reading, in your listening, in your understanding of many things and many people. It can help you to live more fully and humanly—to live with greater consciousness, with increased awareness.

It is essential to realize that the most interesting thing in the entire universe is man. Man is the only creature that builds civilizations or invents dynamos, computers, or rockets; writes histories, laws, poems, notes to the milkman. Man is at the center of all human interests; he has no real substitute. Everything else bears a distinct relationship to him.

It naturally follows that in order to write something meaningful you must consider the relationship of man to your subject, whether that subject is Indian arrowheads, computers, baseball, or your dog Rover. When you write about architecture, you write about man the builder, the shelter seeker. When you write about automobile racing, you write about man's frantic desire to prove that he is better than the machine, that he is still in control of what he has made. When you write about moon rockets, you write about man's courage as he reaches ever farther out in space. Even when you write about particular people, you write about mankind.

## Auxiliary Experiments

1. Make a list of ten novels, short stories, plays, and/or movies which you have especially liked in the past. Go as far back in the past as you want—even to childhood stories or animated cartoons if you are skeptical.

Jot down briefly after the title of each why you like it, as well as you can remember. If you cannot remember, then jot down the general subjects and if possible why the work has "lasted" with you, why its title came to mind. Replace with other titles those which you remember for external reasons, such as "Because I took Lorraine to this movie on our first date."

Then go through the list slowly and list the universals involved in each work. Remember that a universal is usually involved in any struggle, whether the struggle is physical, mental, emotional, or spiritual, or it is the purpose (though perhaps remote) of any struggle. Remember also that a universal is not necessarily pleasant or positive or admirable. Even in the unlikely event that the only literature you have ever enjoyed is animal stories, you will find universals, for the struggles the animal characters engage in have reasons which, though only instinctive, are akin to human motives: this dog is faithful; this wild stallion fights for his mares, or against bondage; this mouse defies the establishmentarian cat.

2.  Leaf through a poetry anthology, preferably (to save time) one with which you are familiar—perhaps the poetry section of your high-school literature textbook. Choose ten poems with varying subjects, preferably poems you know rather well. List the titles, reread the poems, and jot down the universals they treat. Universals are easier to find in lyric poems, but they are as surely present in narrative poems— they make the narratives worth telling. Universals are present in the most ancient and the most modern poetry. If you are an antipoetry person, discovering these for yourself should at least convince you that poetry is not ephemeral.

## UNIVERSALITY AND THE INDIVIDUAL
### MAN AS WRITER

Most student writers feel that an essay, to appeal to its reader, must present a subject that is new, different, even exotic. But the subject you choose or are assigned need not have any of these qualities. Your treatment of it will be unique, if you will allow it to be and if you transmit it accurately, because it will be yours, and you are unique. You want to transmit this uniqueness to a reader who is, after all, unique himself. You need common ground, not novelty, not a gimmick, to transmit this uniqueness. What can be most important is what you do with a subject *before* you begin writing, how you make it relevant to yourself, your reader, and mankind— how you transform it so that it manifests one or more of the universals.

If you can examine an object or experience in its relationship to man and to a universal, the writing you do about it will almost inevitably say something important. The reader's interest and pleasure will follow naturally. You will still face the problem of developing the essay effectively, but you will no longer be wondering whether what you have to say is worth the saying. Because you are a member of the family of man and because you recognize your reader as belonging to the same family, your writing will be natural and meaningful to both you and your reader if it has man at its center. With this insight much of the most difficult part of writing can be done before you have "officially" begun to write.

However, if your memory, your imagination, or your powers of decision are not superhuman, it is a good idea to write little notes to yourself as you think along.

### THE MENTAL WALK IN SEARCH OF IDEAS

One way to discover the subject-man-universal relationship is to take a mental walk around a subject, examine it carefully from as many points of view as possible, associate it with man, and pinpoint any universals that the association reveals.

As I'm writing the first draft of this section I have on my desk a throwaway bottle of Pepsi-Cola. From time to time I take a drink from it. In an hour or so (for I drink the big, economy, sixteen-ounce size) the bottle will be empty. Ten or fifteen minutes later I will become annoyed by the presence of the empty bottle on my desk, take it to the kitchen, and drop it into the container kept there for empty tin cans and throwaway bottles. Tomorrow morning I will empty the container into the large trash can outside. At about nine-thirty Monday morning the trash collector will dump that container into the trash truck, which will haul it some miles away and dump it into an open pit; later a bulldozer will push a layer of dirt over it. Then another layer of trash will be dumped on the same spot, and another layer of dirt will be pushed over it. Is this the end? One quick move, and I'm at a dead end in the city dump! If you merely wanted practice in writing, you could describe the trip of the bottle to the dump, much as I've already done but with more detail. Few, if any, adults would be interested, though you might have the beginnings of a fascinating story for first graders who are still learning about trash trucks, fire trucks, and the like.

Now you are exactly on top of the basic fault of most amateur writing. The little narrative of the throwaway bottle is less than fascinating because it makes no statement about man nor does it even imply anything universal. If you cannot see universality as a basic quality of good writing, you will be writing that which is less than fascinating, less than interesting, less than worth writing. If you cannot now see the lack of universals as a basic fault—read this chapter over from the beginning.

*Persistence with the "barren" subject.* Many times persistence in following a line of thought can help. Centuries after whatever catastrophe may end this civilization, that throwaway bottle will still be resting, perhaps unbroken, in the city dump. With it will be perhaps millions of other throwaway bottles. The design of the bottles may have changed, and the layers of trash will record the change. The dump will preserve the artifacts of the culture—layer upon layer. Perhaps twenty thousand years from now an interplanetary archaeologist, digging through the layers, will lift this bottle from its resting place and make a few shrewd guesses about the kind of people who lived in North America in the twentieth century. One thing will amaze him, no doubt—the hundreds of thousands of glass bottles, part of twenty-seven billion bottles Americans throw away each year. He may even call the Americans the Throwaway Tribes for want of a better description.

Do you see that you can transform a casual observation of a throwaway bottle—a supposedly barren subject—into a much larger and more important observation about people? You can make a statement about people who are living now. You can find something to say about yourself that other people will listen to because it will be about them, too. If you should wish, you could do research and find material for a long article, even a book, about the throwaway people of your time. And this is only one of the myriad subjects that even an empty bottle is filled with.

Sylvia Porter wrote one of her syndicated newspaper articles about what she called "Disposable Everything." She began her thinking not with a cola bottle, but with a Christmas gift catalogue that featured throwaway (disposable) articles. But she used the same process of transformation. Because she writes for the financial pages, she stopped with a description of the articles and a few conclusions about the amount of dis-disposable income the American people "throw away." She did not dwell on human causes and effects.

Among the more fascinating items I've come across in this year's clutch of Christmas catalogs are throwaway sleeping bags at $3.95 apiece, throwaway blankets at $3.50 apiece, throwaway sheets at two for $1.80, throwaway pillowcases costing two for 80¢.

The companies advertising these disposable items obviously are aiming at campers and yachters. But considering today's laundering and dry cleaning costs on top of the initial investments in these items, throwaway sheets and blankets are on the way to becoming bargains for stay-at-homes as well.

But the above already is yesterday's news. Today's "hot" item in the U.S. marketplace is disposable underwear. Bowing in right now are throwaway ladies' underpants made out of nonwoven rayon and costing 15¢ a pair; coming tomorrow are disposable ladies' nightgowns, men's undershorts and ladies' brassieres; and one company is reported going into production in January of porous "breathing" plastic garments costing only pennies each.

Would you have believed only 10 years or so ago, that by 1968, paper dresses would be commonplace and that other paper clothes, ranging from men's dress shirts to baby clothes, bathing suits, ties and raincoats, would be up to a $50 to 100 million a year business?

Would you now believe that in addition to the "linens" and paper clothes we buy today, use briefly and toss into the trash bin, we dispose annually of 321,000 tons of paper napkins, 949,000 tons of paper towels, 340,000 tons of facial tissue, and 1,120,000 tons of toilet paper . . . over one billion dollars' worth of throwaways a year?

And even though you are well aware of the disposable bottle, jar and can, would you accept the estimate that it comes each year to over 27,000,000,000 glass bottles and jars, plus 5,500,000,000 tin cans?

The most rapidly growing segment of the throwaway industry is in disposables for hospitals and other institutions, a clear reflection of our continuing struggle to slow the rising cost of medical care by slashing the cost of hospital services.

In hospitals, disposables now range from sheets and pillowcases to bed clothes, surgical gowns, laboratory coats, bed drapes for non-private facilities, hypodermic needles. . . . disposable hospital kits also are being produced.

To illustrate, there are pre-sterilized surgical packs containing all needed garments for patients, with holes cut out over the body areas in which surgery will take place. There are pre-surgery preparation kits containing disposable razors for shaving, disposable basins for washing, disposable towels. In the offing are disposable plastic thermometers and even "disposable hospital rooms" . . . in the form of plastic balloons which could be blown up inside a hospital room for each new patient, providing his own completely sterile "room."

Clearly, the growing emphasis on convenience in this country, along with the virtual disappearance of household help and the soaring cost of services, is spurring the trend to disposability.

Clearly too, the sharp growth of camping, boating, picnicking and other forms of outdoor recreation have been powerful stimulants to the trend.

And undoubtedly, a fundamental factor has been our mounting total of "throwaway income." Just since 1959, our disposable personal income (i.e., after taxes) has soared from $337 billion to $593 billion.

Our problem in this country is not how to produce enough food and clothing and other items to go around. Our problem in this country is how to throw it away.[5]

This article may be only a point of departure for those who are more concerned about the human values inherent in an entire generation of people willing to spend vast amounts of money for things they plan to throw away after limited use. If you are interested in the sociological or psychological aspects of this growing production and use of disposable merchandise, you can transform the subject again as you try to discover why the throwaway is so acceptable.

*The subject in the dimension of time.* If the bottle of cola on my desk were not a throwaway, I would put it back in its carton ready for the weekly grocery-shopping trip. Then I would haul the cartons out to the car, drive to the grocery

[5] Sylvia Porter, "Disposable Everything." Distributed 1968, Publishers-Hall Syndicate. All rights reserved. Reprinted courtesy of Publishers-Hall Syndicate.

store, unload the cartons into a cart, push the cart into the store, and finally deposit the cartons of empty bottles in the bottle-return bins. This work would take me approximately five extra minutes; for the effort I would earn twelve cents in deposit return. I like to think that the time I save by avoiding such unnecessary work is important to me. When I spend money for things I throw away after one use, I am really buying time. For people, time has become almost as important as money. By producing hundreds of articles that can be used once and then thrown away, manufacturers encourage the desire to save time.

Did Americans always value time as highly as they do now? In the museum are the carefully mended tables and chairs of the pioneers, the knives, scythes, sickles, filed down during innumerable sharpenings to thin strips of steel. The pioneers did the opposite of what I do: they traded *time* for a new back to the rocking chair, a new leg on the table, a new handle for the axe.

Why am I willing to trade things for time when my ancestors were not? The continuing industrial revolution provides at least part of the answer. As the machines took over the doing, and even much of the thinking that precedes it, *things* became relatively inexpensive. Raw materials are everywhere for the machines to dig out, to transport, to process, and to manufacture into *things* of plastic, ceramic, metal, glass. Materials there are in God's plenty—but time? I have a bit more time than my grandfather had, for life expectancy has risen. But time is a deceitful thing and may come to an end suddenly, for you or for me as it did for our ancestors. The moment something becomes scarce, or seems to be scarce, it becomes valuable; so it is with time. I want to hoard every bit of it, and so I trade things for time—and will probably increase the pace of the trading with every passing year.

*The "empty" subject as container.* Up to this point in your mental walk around an empty bottle, you have not considered what it once contained, a liquid that pleased the taste. Your question is "How do I transform the taste of a liquid into a subject that will be fundamentally interesting?" Associate the taste with man, develop some kind of relationship between taste and man. Man likes to taste.

A look about will convince you that man is always tasting— table food, water, soft drinks, hard drinks, candy, gum, smoke. People never seem to be happy unless they are nibbling, sucking, sipping, pulling smoke through their mouths and lungs, or in some way tasting something. And suddenly you realize that you do have another subject out of the Pepsi bottle—man the taster. Of course man is not the only animal with a sense of taste. Television commercials insist that certain combinations of liver, chicken, fish, and horsemeat have more appeal for cats and dogs than do other combinations of the same foods. But most animals stop eating when they have enough. Man is the only animal that has made tasting a way of life.

*The origins of the subject.* To continue the mental walk, consider how the bottle itself is made. A machine pours molten glass into forms and spits out thousands of identical bottles every hour. Another machine may box the bottles, seal the boxes, and load them into trucks. Where is man in this process? He has been almost totally divorced from the machine process and has no actual work to do with his muscles. Separated from the labor that once gave him the feel of accomplishment, the muscular feel, is this mere dial watcher now in search of a substitute for the muscular movement that he both resented and enjoyed? Must he now find some process to give him a substitute for the muscular relief he is denied at a job that requires no exertion? Might that substitute take the form of sipping soft drinks or coffee, chewing gum, nibbling candy, smoking cigarettes one after the other?

Take still another look at the empty Pepsi bottle. It is made of glass, one of man's first plastics. Could you now find a universal connection between glass and man? Could man's use of glass give some insight into the phenomenon of man? How many ways does he use it? He uses it to hold the most virulent of poisons, the most healing of drugs, the most delicate of perfumes. As crystal it is serviceable yet fragile beauty for his use and enjoyment. Stained glass has inspired him to visions of God. The telescope lens brings distant objects close to his eye, compressing his universe; the lens of the microscope, on the other hand, explodes it.

*The subject as problem.* Some practical souls, of course, would rather do something about bottles than write about them. Perhaps Dr. Samuel F. Hulbert of Clemson University was taking a mental walk around an empty cola bottle on his desk when he realized that city dumps would soon be filled with bottles:

> [Dr. Hulbert] is developing a self-destroying bottle, that, when broken, will turn soft and melt away.
> The trouble with our present "disposable" bottles is that they really aren't. They have to be disposed of somehow—and since each American uses an average of 135 glass containers a year, the disposal problem is becoming literally mountainous. Some place has to be found to dump about eighty million bottles and jars every day; and, as nearly every municipality has discovered, this chore is both expensive and unsightly.
> Dr. Hulbert believes that he can create a new kind of glass which will begin to hydrolyze as soon as it is broken —that is, to react with the moisture in the air so that it becomes flexible and eventually turns into a puddle of water.[6]

Other people, of course, simply don't discard bottles:

> The French, by the way, handle such matters better, and more simply. The very thought of throwing away a bottle grates on their thrifty souls. Consequently, French wine sellers charge a whopping deposit on every one, with the result that nearly all of them promptly come back to the shop. Thus they save money on trash disposal—and I have never seen an empty bottle lying by a French roadside.[7]

The Swedes have another answer to the problem—a beer bottle made of paper and plastics. Lying on a roadside,

---

[6] John Fischer, "The Easy Chair: Christmas List," *Harper's Magazine,* CCXXXVII (December, 1968), 18. Copyright © 1968, by Harper's Magazine, Inc. Reprinted by permission of the author.
[7] *Ibid.,* p. 20.

it will decompose in sunlight; buried in a dump, it will be dissolved by acids in the soil. Tossed in the fire, it will burn.

## THE IMPOSED SUBJECT

Yet perhaps you are sitting at your desk, sweating in the white glow of the study lamp, and muttering to yourself, "So now I know how to find a subject and make it interesting. So today Fogey *gives* the class a subject and says to write on that—just that. Now what do I do?"

And what *can* you do if, for example, your instructor is incredibly 1850—a nature lover who has been reading the romantics so long he thinks Emerson is still alive? What if he decides that you will write a composition about nature?

*Possibilities within prescribed limits.* Is the subject really so difficult? Actually, the instructor is permissive: he is allowing you to choose your own predication. Although the general subject of your essay must be nature, you can write anything you wish about it and still fulfill the assignment. The subject may be his, but the possibilities are yours.

Before you go slogging through the woods looking for these possibilities to choose from, predicate upon, and transform (you're remembering that the romantics found inspiration in the woods), try a vicarious look at nature.

Check the dictionary to see whether the word *nature* itself will give you any possibilities. (You'll feel less like a victim the moment you see choices; you'll not be distracted by self-pity, which is a great consumer of time.) College dictionaries give the word *nature* about ten separate definitions. Some of the definitions do not pertain to the kind of nature that your instructor and his friend Emerson have in mind. Of those remaining, you consider for no special reason (you have to start somewhere!) the broadest one: "the entire physical universe."

According to this definition of nature, your subject is the universe and everything in it. The world is nature. The people in the world, other than yourself, are nature. Exclude yourself because the self is, for present purposes, you as writer. Thus you see that you'd better narrow the subject if you're not going to spend the rest of your life writing about it.

So, as a start, you narrow it to the obvious, the easily observable, common things that the average person thinks of as nature, the green, growing things—plants, grasses, trees. Now the hope of discovering a writable relationship between the subject and the experiences of man becomes real.

But what relationship? What, if anything, does man have in common with grass, trees, weeds? Or can you write something about what he does *not* have in common with them? Can you show how he is different from them? Can you contrast him and them? Contrast is a relationship. Can you find some universal basis on which to contrast man and a tree, a bush, a weed?

*The walk.* Perhaps now is the time for a walk, a mental or physical walk until you come to the first weed, flower, or clump of grass that has escaped the mower. Look closely at it. A single plant may have hundreds of seeds clinging to it or blowing from it. A large tree may have tens of thousands of seeds. All about you, now that you are looking for something, you see thousands, millions, billions of seeds—and suddenly you become aware of a contrast which has universal meaning. Nature spreads her seeds by billions and allows them to fall where they may, to grow if they fall upon good ground, to sprout and wither away if they fall upon the sterile rock. Nature is careless and prodigal. This prodigality seems to be the fixed and definite plan by which nature survives.

And what of man? In his stumbling way, man attempts to apply reason to his method of survival. He tries to plan his life, to bring order to it, by structuring it according to the ways that have seemed most successful in the past. He sets up moral and ethical stop-and-go signs to regulate the spreading of his seed and the behavior of the life he brings into the world. Do you have a manageable contrast now? Could it be nature's emphasis upon unlimited reproduction and man's drive for an ordered life? It involves man. It has a universal basis. You can write an essay.

The following essay is the result of a process like the one you have just been through; the writer, a night-school student at a Midwestern university.

### The Order of Nature

Although some find in nature a unity, an order, and a plan, I can no longer look upon it without being overwhelmed by the enormous carelessness with which it goes about its primary business of reproduction. Everywhere is profligacy; everywhere the odds for survival operate on a scale so gigantic as to be almost unthinkable. Everywhere are birth and death, growth out of decay; but over all, and in all, and beneath all is the subdued roar of birth, birth, life, life, survive, survive, survive!

Last week I trimmed along my fence line, rooting out hundreds of six-inch seedlings of the tree of heaven that towers in my neighbor's yard. Appalled by the wasted energy, the fruitfulness of nature, I bent my back to the work of uprooting, knowing full well that I was fighting against built-in odds, fighting the bursting seeds, the wind, the rain, and the warmth of the sun. Clear a little thread-like line I could, but to dent the plan, to block out the vision of a universe totally absorbed in reproduction, my efforts were but the shadow of a fantasy, and I saw myself alone, puny, far weaker than the seedlings even now lying on the grass, their roots drying in the hot sunlight. But finally I was finished, and as I looked along the clean fence line I knew

Tension develops as the idea of unity, order, and plan is contrasted with the idea of enormous carelessness.

Birth and death set up another contrast.

Repetition lends emphasis.

The illustration shows the limitations of man in an almost primitive fight against nature.

The listing of concrete details is an effective means of gaining realism.

The smallness of the task com-

vaguely that I had brought a kind of order to a wild disorder of elemental forces.

Later that evening I walked down the street past the house with the unkempt yard where pigweeds and seedlings of the tree of heaven grew uncut from one month's end to another. In the yard a stripling tree, too thick of trunk for mower or sickle, sprang from beside the old stone foundation and pushed its way toward the roofline of the cottage. One that survived, I said to myself and stopped to look at the seed clusters already hanging thick from the branches. Then I moved on quickly, for in the dark recesses of the porch I saw nature working not with trees or grasses, weeds or flowers, but with man; and at the nearness of it, the associations that had followed me all that afternoon and evening moved me more profoundly than ever.

Against the farther wall of the porch stood two youngsters, boy and girl, locked in each other's arms. I knew them, of course: She, barely fifteen, with tight short shorts, scanty blouse, long blond hair carelessly combed. He, sixteen, if that, skintight Levis, shirtless in the warm night air, his yellow hair curled at the back of his neck. They stood there motionless, unaware of anything but the pulse that beat between them and that locked them together with straining arms and crushed mouths.

pleted contrasts with the grossness of nature's carelessness.

The second illustration, which contrasts with the first, shows how nature operates in man as well as in plant life. Note the detail: *pigweeds, seedlings, stripling tree, seed clusters.* Note also the repetition of key words. The use of the word *stripling* to describe *tree* allows the reader to make a vital comparison with the teen-agers in the following paragraph.

Describing the teen-agers as motionless helps to equate man and vegetation. This paragraph moves quickly to show nature working in man. The writer's acquaintance with the youngsters allows him to describe them in the dim light of the porch without violation of his point of view. The details of clothing and physical appearance make the description vivid.

Nature, careless and prodigal, an immense force, surges through vine and vein, spreading its seeds widely, wildly, intent only on survival; and we are part of that force, yet through some faint law of our own being or making, we strain against it to bring order to a plan that of itself knows no order. And suddenly my fence line became startlingly important in that soft June night; for it was order, it was demarcation, it was a force against force; and I knew as I had never known before the the position of man in a universe of procreant urges powerful beyond measure and belief.

Here is a summing up with word repetition: *Careless, prodigal, force,* and *survival* help to knit the essay together.

The use of *vine* and *vein,* followed by *widely* and *wildly,* shows the forces at work in nature to be the forces at work in man also. The repetition of *fence line* serves two purposes. It indicates man's striving for order and shows that man's efforts are almost futile against the procreant urges of nature.

## Auxiliary Experiments

### I

1.  Try taking mental walks around the following:

> crack in plaster
> deodorant
> ashtray
> termites
> dead cockroach
> salt shaker
> shoe

2.  Work out several subject-man-universal relationships with each.

3.  Without moving from your chair, look about you and find other things to take mental walks around.

### II

Leaf through any sales catalogue (from a department store, a specialty shop, a mail-order house, etc.) until at least one subject-man-universal relationship occurs to you. For example, a toy catalogue can give rise to many such relationships bearing on custom, culture, taste, economics, competition, ingenuity, temptation, greed.

## STREAM OF CONSCIOUSNESS AS SOURCE

Almost any book, magazine, or newspaper can supply you with hundreds of ideas for essays your own experience has already prepared you to write.

For example, read any newspaper article as you would normally read it. Then read it again, and this time concentrate not so much on the meaning of the article itself as on the fringe meanings—what any part (statement, phrase, even single word) suggests to you. Let your mind play with these fringe meanings, and using a stream-of-consciousness [8] technique jot down every question or thought or association that occurs to you, no matter how unrelated or even ridiculous it may seem at the moment. As soon as the possibilities of that part seem exhausted, move on to the next part—keep jotting as steadily as you can. Do not concern yourself yet with the feasibility of developing an essay from any of these thoughts and associations. If you stop them for judgment as they arrive, they will stop arriving.

This very serious game is not necessarily solitaire—any number can play. When two or more people participate, it becomes a brainstorming session. Furthermore, it can be played with any object, subject, or idea—or with the utter lack of an idea for the solution of a particular problem.

The next step is to go through the notes you've jotted down and turn as many as you can into statements, each of which in-

[8] You are concerned here, of course, with stream of consciousness not as a literary technique nor as a means of presenting character and events to a reader. You will employ it quite differently, as a technique of discovering your own ideas through the associations, memories, mental images, thoughts, and emotional reactions which occur spontaneously when you consider the ideas of others, ideas in this case presented in a newspaper article. (It is possible, of course, that when you read your stream-of-consciousness jottings you will gain insight into yourself, just as if you were reading a stream-of-consciousness story in which you yourself were the central character.)

volves the subject, man, and a universal. Often you will find that widely separated associations will combine readily into such statements. Then the choices and the rejections begin. Choose those that seem to lend themselves to development in essay form. From among them, choose those that are most interesting and appropriate to *you* as a writer.

The following newspaper article is partially worked out according to the above procedure. The text is accompanied by the stream-of-consciousness jottings of one person, who was reading the article for the second time.

### Medical Role Proposed for Rural Ministers

COLUMBUS:—(AP) A speaker with a background in ministry and medicine yesterday told a pastors' gathering here that clergymen must have a dual role, succeeding where organized medicine has not.

Dr. Granger E. Westberg of Wittenberg University proposed a new concept of using rural churches as medical clinics in his address during the final day of the annual Ohio Pastors convocation, which began Monday.

Is he a medical missionary? Medical missionaries go to underdeveloped countries. Might they stay in the United States? Where would they be? Appalachia? Rural South? The Navajos? The Eskimos? A convention for clergymen. Why not? What wild times they must have! Has organized medicine tried? How do you organize medicine?

How could you have a clinic in a church? Move out the Ladies' Aid Society suppers—take over Sunday school rooms. After communion, please file through the X-ray mobile unit. Back it up to the church door, and nobody's allowed to leave except through the truck. You could sing hymns standing in line. Everybody knows where the church is. Plenty of parking spaces around rural churches. No problem to park your car—or your mule. The Ladies' Aid Society could cook for the patients. The building is already there. Churches are empty—most of them—six days out of seven. Of course pastors' conventions have to begin on Monday—can't skip church on Sunday like the rest of us.

He said he has had the idea for years. But only recently, he said, has the American Medical Association (AMA) admitted that at least 20 million Americans are not receiving proper care. Most of them, the AMA found, are in rural areas.

20,000,000. Too many. One would be too many. What's proper medical care? What you need, whether you want it or not? What you need *when* you need it? What if you don't think you need it? Or know you need it? What if nobody in the whole county wants it? What about superstition? Whose fault? Ignorance? Probably. Grandma remembers hearing of babies dying of "summer complaint" and nobody asking what that was or questioning why they got it. If they died in winter, what was it? Ignorance. Ignorance like a blanket over the country—over the cities, too—over the whole country. Not just then. Now. Still. What if you had appendicitis and good old Granny gave you sulphur and molasses or whatever it is? What if you broke your leg and there was no one to come—or go to? But you couldn't go with a broken leg. No ambulances, either, of course. Do ambulances go very far into the hills? Some places without roads. Helicopters? The helicopter lands in the churchyard. Country churches surrounded by cemeteries. Strange to wake up being carried through a cemetery.

Dr. Westberg's plan has church buildings being put to use each day of the week, staffed with persons trained in medicine or counseling. Nonmedical staff members would be at least as important as doctor-physicians, since Dr. Westberg feels spiritual discomfort often causes ills ostensibly physical.

Each day of the week—I'm ahead of you—I already thought of that. Where do these "persons" come from? How do you get them out of their soft offices in cities? How do you get them out of their soft city offices into the city slums? How do I know they have soft offices? Or offices? Who are they? Are there any extra ones? Great idea for ex-Peace Corps personnel in cultural shock. Great training for Peace Corps? Training already set up. The U.S. already has a domestic Peace Corps—VISTA—things like that. Not enough, of course. As usual. Not enough good people. Not enough people want to help. Not enough love. Not enough people will give. Not enough people want to. Not enough know how to give, how to love. Be careful, Doc—you'll talk yourself out of medical personnel. That's for Aunt Elsie, though, the old hypochondriac. *Ostensibly* obviously healthy as a truck driver. But she doesn't think so. Not her spirit, it's in her mind, really. What's the difference, exactly? Is peace of mind spiritual? I can see the nonmedical personnel pulling rank. They'd have to put up a sign, signed by Dr. Westberg. Maybe "God loveth a cheerful nonmedical staff member at least as much as a doctor-physician." Cross-stitch.

"People in rural areas need—really need—somebody to talk with," Dr. Westberg explained in a news conference.[9]

The loneliness of the rural area. The shack, all by itself. No phone. Even the ranchers, miles from the next ranch. But they have helicopters and palomino horses—not all of them, of course. Maybe not many. Rural poor, like urban poor. But they go to town for provisions. How often? What would you buy if you just went to town once a month? The sod huts a hundred years ago, covered with snow drifts. You can't see out the windows. Nobody to talk to—can't even get out for weeks. Trappers. The women. Women need somebody to talk to, to talk to them. They need society more than men do and get less of it, really, even in cities maybe. Maybe not. They leave the dishes and go gossip. Kaffee klatsch. But what if there's nobody to go see, whether or not she does her housework? Sod hut housework. Sod housework. Sod hutwork. How do you kill

[9] "Medical Role Proposed for Rural Ministers," Dayton *Journal Herald*, January 30, 1969, p. 27. Reprinted by permission of The Associated Press.

germs in a sod hut? How can you be antiseptic in a shack? There's nobody to see, except over the mountain. On foot, and maybe you're sick. And no phone. The farm wife working in the field with her husband to keep from going mad, from beating her head against the wall, the sod wall of the sod house. Frost's poem about the runaway wife. The suicide rate among sodbusters' wives must have been high. What about sodbusters without wives? What is the suicide rate in Appalachia? What makes you want to kill yourself? How would it be to want to die? How is mental health (nice, quiet, sterile term) in Appalachia? But you can be lonely when you're in a room with a hundred people. You can be lonely at a party. Can't show it, though. Never show it. Is it worse to be lonely when you're not alone? When you're alone, then you can't help it. You can't think there must be something wrong with you that you're lonely. You don't have to worry about that. You at least know why you're lonely. There's nobody there. What if the baby is dying, and there's no help? And then you have to dig the baby's grave, while your wife watches. What if the sodbuster is dying, and there's a blizzard?

## Auxiliary Experiments

1. Work out stream-of-consciousness notes for three or more of the remaining paragraphs of the article:

> While the doctor-minister would have to have a medical degree, he would be something of a "wholistic physician."
>
> He was asked if the AMA might oppose such a concept, feeling a threat to physicians' livelihood.
>
> "The recent AMA admission about 20 million people shows the doctors realize something must be done. If the plan

brought church-clinic facilities to nice suburbs, the AMA might very well oppose it."

The person in charge of healing the body as well as the spirit, Dr. Westberg said, would receive a fraction of an average physician's fee.

"He would get the salary of a medical missionary or a pastor of a large church. This is about $15,000 a year."

The University of Chicago pioneered in the dual-role concept when it appointed Dr. Westberg to both the medical and theological faculties in 1956.

He was called a "professor of medicine and religion."

Since, he has been at the Texas Medical Center and at Baylor University College of Medicine with the same functions. Dr. Westberg now is professor of practical theology and director of continuing education at the Hamma School of Theology, Wittenberg University, in Springfield.

A list of books by Dr. Westberg appears to show his interest: Minister and Doctor Meet, Community Psychiatry and The Clergyman, and Nurse, Pastor and Patient.

He is uncertain of pastors' reactions to his proposal yesterday. Others in the fields of ministry and medicine have been receptive, he said, and he is optimistic.[10]

2. Discuss in class, in the manner of a brainstorming session, three or more of the remaining paragraphs in the article. Record the session on tape, or take notes.

3. From among the jottings on the first six paragraphs of the article, develop statements of the subject-man-universal relationship.

4. From your own jottings or the tape or notes of the brainstorming session, develop statements according to the subject-man-universal formula.

5. Discuss the statements you produced in 3 and/or 4 as suitable for the development of essays.

6. Choose any article from your local or campus newspaper and make stream-of-consciousness notes. Develop statements involving subject-man-universal relationships.

[10] *Ibid.*

# The Thesis

You may have noticed that both Tom Wolfe and the author of "The Order of Nature" kept carefully to the subjects they were presenting. Both authors chose from among what must have been hundreds of closely allied impressions only those that suited their purpose, that supported the points they wanted to make. In thinking through their subjects, both authors stayed within carefully defined, self-imposed limitations and at the same time developed and expanded their ideas until those ideas became entities in themselves. In doing so, they worked from the basic writing concept of *thesis*, that goes back at least as far as the great classical lectures on the art of rhetoric.

## WHAT A THESIS IS

A thesis is a statement formulated as a result of an insight into a problem being examined. A thesis is a promise to the reader, which the essay fulfills. It is a proposition, which the writer carries out, or defends. It is an implied question, which the essay answers. It is a challenge—to the reader to see a subject as the writer does; to the writer to make the reader see, make him understand. It is a seed, from which the essay grows. A thesis can be supported, defended, maintained, developed, argued, amplified, in writing or in speech.

## HOW A THESIS FUNCTIONS

For example, in a store window you see a pair of shoes that you would like to buy. You move closer and see the price tag. The price is far more than you thought it would be, yet the shoes are so attractive that you consider buying them.

You make a rapid inventory of the money you have and the money you have coming during the next two weeks. You compute your expenses for the next two weeks. If you bought the shoes, you would have to go without recreation and a number of necessities as well. You gain a sudden insight into

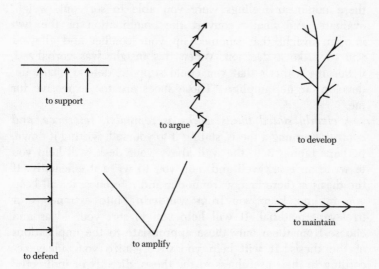

Figure 1.  Using the Thesis

your problem and say to yourself, "Those shoes are too expensive for me." A half block farther on you meet a friend, and together you go back to look at the shoes. You repeat your statement about the shoes. If your friend questions your decision, you can support it: "If I bought them, I wouldn't have enough money left to eat next week"; defend it: "Shoes of that quality would make the rest of my clothes look shabby"; develop it: "I would have to forgo doing things that I enjoy if I were to buy those shoes"; argue it: "I would be living beyond my means"; amplify it: "Such an expenditure would keep me broke, absolutely broke with no money for any emergencies."

You didn't write an essay about these shoes because another mode of communication—speech—satisfied both your audience and you. But you could have written an essay because you had a thesis: "Those shoes are too expensive for me."

In the beginning your problem was completely nonlinear, an amorphous mass of feelings about the joys of owning and wearing an especially attractive pair of shoes. Only after an analysis of the linear realities of your finances as opposed to these nonlinear feelings were you able to sort out, weigh, evaluate, and finally convert the combination of the two into an insight that summed up your conflict and allowed you to make a decision. When this insight was verbalized, it became a thesis that you could support, defend, maintain, develop, argue, amplify: "Those shoes are too expensive for me."

*A clearly stated thesis works as reminder, reference, and control.* Forming a thesis, stating it to yourself, writing it down, perhaps taping it to the wall above your desk, will help you to write an essay well and help you to write it efficiently. If the thesis is there first, as reminder and reference, it will keep you in line, keep you from wandering into extraneous or irrelevant material. It will help you to sort your ideas and choose from them only those appropriate to the implications of the thesis. It will help you to organize your ideas according to their usefulness to the thesis, directly or indirectly. It will filter your ideas and clarify them. It will, in sum, make your insight viable by enabling you to communicate it. In all of these ways, the thesis, even while it commands, serves.

Your summer job comes to an end a week before you thought it would. During the long drive home you make plans. You decide to keep the first day all to yourself, starting it with a swim in Bush Lake, your favorite swimming spot during those beautiful years before you had to spend your vacations working.

The next morning your young brother sees you with your swim fins and asks where you're going. At your reply, "Bush Lake," he laughs. Bush Lake, he says, is so polluted that no one has dared to swim in it for two years. You are astounded. Polluted! The word becomes real. You remember skimming over magazine and newspaper articles about pollution, but always they told of other lakes, of rivers far from your city. Your astonishment turns into an anger that a day in the municipal swimming pool cannot dampen. You wonder whether every river and lake in the country is polluted. Who is responsible? Why doesn't somebody do something?

That evening you decide that you will do something to force public attention upon the growing national problem of

pollution. You'll write a letter to the editor of the daily newspaper. Thousands of people will read the letter; some of them
may be inspired to act. As you sit at your desk, you are en-
couraged that into your mind comes a flood of things to write,
the ramifications, the implications, the almost endless projec-
tions of your subject. You jot down a few of the reasons
why pollution of lakes and rivers must be stopped.

> Many lakes and rivers are already unfit for swimming, fishing,
> and boating.
> Vacationers can no longer enjoy camping trips.
> Pollution will destroy the sources of pure water upon which
> towns and cities depend.
> Wildlife will be poisoned.
> The balance of nature will be upset.
> Property along lakeshores and river fronts will deteriorate
> rapidly.
> Rivers will become carriers of corruption and disease.
> Polluted rivers will pollute the oceans and eventually eliminate
> them as future sources of food for man.

You are amazed at how easily the list grows. You will let
the public know. You will force action! Enthusiastically you
read the directions to correspondents of the "Letters to the
Editor" section in the newspaper. You are startled to learn
that letters must be limited to three hundred words. If your
letter is longer, the editor, an unsympathetic stranger, will
cut it for you. If you were to include all the points you have
already jotted down, you would not be able to develop any
of them.

As you look over your list again, you realize this time that
almost everyone who can read a newspaper must already
know these general facts about water pollution. You must
rifle in on only one aspect of the subject and present that aspect as vividly as you can. You try to formulate a main idea
upon which your letter will concentrate, a thesis which it
can develop. You begin, "Water pollution must be stopped
before all our lakes and rivers are poisoned." The sentence is
a catchall. You try again. "Water pollution will soon eliminate
our sources of pure water." Far too general for three hundred
words. "Water pollution is a crime against the next genera-

tion." Better, but still general; to develop that one adequately, you'd have to marshal more arguments than you have space for. By now you are almost as disgusted with yourself as you are with those who have allowed water pollution to continue. But, try as you may, you cannot seem to find a thesis that three hundred words can do justice to. You quit for the evening; tomorrow you'll try again.

The next morning, still angry with those who polluted the nation's water supply and those who didn't stop them, you decide that a trip to Bush Lake may inspire you. You drive to the lake, kick off your shoes, and wade into the dark-green water. You notice that a thin, oily substance clings to your feet and legs. You wipe it off and notice a blackish-brown stain on your towel. So this is pollution! With your shoes on again, you walk along the shoreline. The private swimming rafts are gone; the wooden piers around which the little sailboats clustered are falling into the lake. Dead fish float in the shallows. Ahead of you a concrete storm sewer spews a slimy fluid into the water. As you move closer, a fat brown rat pokes his head out of the sewer, looks at you, and scurries back. Your anger grows as you walk along. Within two hours you have found five storm sewers dumping their putrid liquid into the lake. Rats scamper in and out of them. The whole thing is absurd! The rats have taken over Bush Lake! With a sudden insight you know that you will write not about water pollution in general, not about water pollution over the entire nation, but about storm-sewer pollution, rat pollution, at Bush Lake. Here is a thesis you can handle in 300 words: "This town has turned Bush Lake over to the rats."

No discussion of thesis is realistic without consideration of time and space limitations. In freshman English, you are expected to write compositions that will probably vary in length from 300 to 1,000 words. This space limitation is inescapable. Time limitations imposed by the pressures of other courses are equally inescapable. To write 700 words, each of which fits nicely into the context of the other 699, takes time. If only in self-defense, you must limit the length of your papers. A thesis that can be adequately developed in 5,000 words is not a thesis for a 700-word paper. If you limit the thesis, you need not curtail its development. The thesis must be adjusted, limited to a statement that can be developed in 700 words, or the composition will be a congested mass of obvious generalities.

For example, "Exploring the Moon" is pure subject, without predication of any kind. This subject would require volumes for even a general treatment. The first step is to change the subject into a statement that says something about exploring the moon. "Exploring the moon should be given the highest American priority" predicates something about the subject, but to develop the predication the writer would have to support his statement against all the claims that could be advanced for any and all other competing American "priorities." A listing of a few of the possible American priorities shows the magnitude of the job:

> Rebuilding the cities
> Creating effective mass transportation
> Finding cures for heart disease, cancer, etc.
> Overcoming air, water, and soil contamination
> Providing adequate food, clothing, and shelter for the underprivileged
> Providing equal educational opportunities for everyone
> Controlling organized crime
> Providing adequate care for the mentally ill
> Preserving natural resources
> Converting prisons into rehabilitation centers

By a process of elimination you develop a much more specialized statement: "Exploring the moon is more important than rebuilding our cities." After thinking of that statement for a few minutes you realize that you can't do justice to it in seven hundred words. You ask yourself, "In what ways is it more important?" And then you wonder whether *important* is the word you really mean. You recall the excitement of the first landing, when everyone in America seemed enthralled. The moon landing did give all Americans a common interest. Your statement now becomes "Exploring the moon would give Americans a greater sense of unity than would rebuilding the cities." You have again narrowed the subject.

You undoubtedly noticed that as the subject narrowed it

changed from the big one you really wanted to discuss to the much smaller one you could do justice to in seven hundred words. Have you actually lost the opportunity of saying anything important? Not really. If, within the space limitations available to you, you were to attempt one of the larger, much more inclusive subjects, you could not avoid the big, general statements that you know are only boiled-down expressions of the thinking of others, oversimplifications. You wouldn't have space for supporting evidence of any kind. You wouldn't make anything clearer to your reader than it had been before. But, when you limit the thesis, you can give it unlimited development.

Try thinking of your subject as a vast room, filled with a thousand girls, each of them a potential thesis, all of them talking at once. Heard together, they make only a meaningless clamor. Choose one girl from the thousand, the one most attractive to you, separate her from the mass, draw her out, and she will say fascinating things. Thus you must separate your special thesis from the mass of others if either you or the reader is to get any real meaning from it.

## HOW A THESIS EVOLVES

The stimulus to thesis may enter the mind as a nonlinear, rather amorphous impression; from its interaction with knowledge already stored there an insight develops, but the insight too may be nonlinear. The insight becomes a possible thesis as soon as you force it into linearity by putting it into words, into a statement that seems adequate to you and probably understandable to others. Once clearly verbalized, the statement is subject to logical consideration, as a result of which you may find it necessary to add to it, subtract from it, or rephrase it. But since you can examine it only after you have verbalized it, the statement (now potential thesis) operates to limit its own development to those ideas inherent in it. These, then, are the steps in thesis formation:

1.  Stimulus enters the mind as a sensation (nonlinear).
2.  Sensation plus previous knowledge equals insight (still nonlinear).

3. Nonlinear insight verbalized equals linear insight equals possible thesis statement.
4. Possible thesis statement plus logical analysis equals potential thesis statement.
5. Potential thesis statement adjusted to time and space limitations equals probable thesis statement.

## Auxiliary Experiments

Find at least one thesis in each of the following:

Should the conscientious-objector regulations exempt those who object to a particular war?

If a young man finds he can support himself by working only ten hours a week, is he justified in doing nothing the rest of the week?

Does the air-conditioned apartment destroy any community of interest among neighboring apartment dwellers?

Prisons and reformatories have been described as human warehouses. Discuss.

Discuss the unwillingness of most Americans to do more than talk about air and water pollution.

Discuss the use of listening devices and wire tapping.

Does American individualism prevent the successful use of mass transportation?

Discuss the computer as management.

Discuss the influence of liberal arts graduates and undergraduates upon American life.

# CHAPTER III

# From Subject to Thesis –and On to the Essay

## Impression, Insight, Thesis

An essay is not a direct result of a single sense impression. It develops through a series of steps in which the impression that sparks the process combines with old experiences stored in the mind and results in an insight which in turn generates the thesis.

### THE IMPRESSION IN ISOLATION

Because it is natural to concentrate first upon those impressions that shout for attention (they may of course be important in themselves), you may become absorbed in them and forget the search for insight. As a consequence, you may merely record, become the camera. Or, in attempting to gain insight, you may be overinfluenced by the interpretations of others and only echo them.

For example, disorders on college campuses may tempt the observer to take over the job of the camera and/or to allow the interpretations of others to substitute for his own insight. What shouts for attention is the students' overt acts of defiance and the authorities' use of force: the physical violence, the destruction of campus property, the loaded paddy wagons; the bricks, rocks, and insults hurled, the tear gas thrown and sprayed. The clubbed student, the policeman who caught the brick in his mouth may find message enough in the medium. Others, not physically involved, must look for meaning beyond as well as within the action.

## COMBINING NEW EXPERIENCE AND OLD KNOWLEDGE

Congressman Charles W. Whalen, Jr., examined the campus disorders (1) by direct observation, (2) through the eyes of other observers, and (3) on the basis of his own experience as university professor and department chairman. Here, in an excerpt from the speech which developed, he summarizes some of the observations of others:

> Campus disorders have been attributed to several causes. Some observers have stressed the concern of our youth with our Vietnam involvement. Others emphasize the backlash generated by the inequities in our Selective Service System. Reaction against racial discrimination is often cited as a source of student unrest. Finally some ascribe distortion of our national values as a primary reason for student disenchantment.[1]

Congressman Whalen compared these observations with his own knowledge of university administrations, faculties, and students and with the history of American higher education. The combination of new experience and old knowledge resulted in many insights, among them those in the following excerpt:

> Our nation's universities are now the one nongovernmental institution whose authoritarian structure has undergone little or no change. Relationships between administration and faculty, faculty and student, are much the same today as they were two centuries ago.

[1] Charles W. Whalen, Jr., "Student Unrest," address at the commencement exercises of Stivers High School, Dayton, Ohio, June 5, 1969, inserted at the request of Hon. Richard S. Schweiker of Pennsylvania in Congressional Record, June 17, 1969, p. E4977.

On many campuses, for example, a faculty member can be dismissed without cause at the end of his contract period. In many instances promotion and tenure decisions are arbitrarily made and are not appealable.

Student needs frequently are subrogated by professors who must adhere to the doctrine of "publish or perish." The quality of undergraduate instruction sometimes is sacrificed on the altar of prestige-seeking graduate programs.

Curricula are developed with little consideration of the requirements of those whom courses of instruction are intended to benefit. A college education is the only commodity in the market place whose buyer pays $12,000 and has absolutely no voice in what he is to receive.

From the foregoing it can be concluded that the "autocratic authority" still is the order of the day on many of our college campuses. From my own experience I realize that there is nothing malicious in this posture. For instance, as a department chairman it just never occurred to me that it might be productive to invite students to participate in departmental faculty meetings. Yet, today this is being done! What I am saying is that it is human to accept the status quo until circumstances dictate otherwise.[2]

Congressman Whalen ran the impressions of campus disorders through the records of previous experience and knowledge in his mind to arrive at the insight from which he developed his thesis: "Today's student unrest will disappear only with a change in the manner in which authority is exercised."

## Auxiliary Experiments

1.   Treat Congressman Whalen's analysis as you would any new impression. Combine it with your own experience and knowledge. Does the resulting insight permit you to extend any part of the analysis?

2.   Consider any part of his analysis in relation to the high school(s) you are familiar with. Is an analysis of a college situation applicable to a high-school one? For example, to what extent could high-school students determine their own curricula?

[2] *Ibid.,* p. E4978.

# What May Happen in the Mind of the Writer

Perhaps you are familiar with the chemist's symbolic model of a molecule, composed of tens of little balls fastened together by thin rods. If the chemist introduces another element or other elements into the molecule represented by his model, a new molecule will form, and he must change the arrangement of the model to conform to its properties. The records of previous experience and knowledge transformed into insights and understandings in the mind of the writer can be imagined as similar three-dimensional configurations, generally spherical though not solid, each made up of numerous smaller spheres (representing individual bits of information) loosely linked together. These cluster not necessarily because the mind has deliberately arranged them together but because they relate to one another through similarity or some other association. When an important new sense image touches such a configuration, the balance of the latter is upset, with the result that it undergoes a radical change in arrangement—in meaning.

For example, you may be lukewarm about children until one day you see a father shouting at his seven-year-old boy, who has left his tricycle in the driveway. You see the angry father, the upraised hand, the trembling child cowering in fear as he moves slowly toward the tricycle, then tries to run with it onto the lawn, and finally stumbles, falls, and lies sobbing on the grass. Your sudden insight into the problem of the defenseless child faced by overwhelming force results in a change in attitude that might be illustrated in Figure 2.

Figure 2, of course, is a simplification. A new impression or series of impressions may start a chain reaction involving any number of configurations. After the shifting and changing are complete, entirely new configurations will represent any new insights so arrived at.

This shifting and changing can be imagined as occurring when a writer gropes for an insight. The right sense image attaches itself to a previously constructed configuration, a chain reaction takes place, and a new configuration—an in-

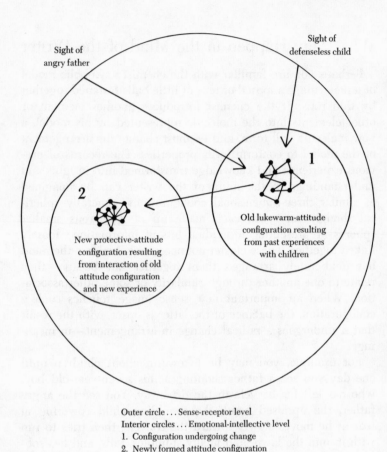

Outer circle ... Sense-receptor level
Interior circles ... Emotional-intellective level
1. Configuration undergoing change
2. Newly formed attitude configuration

Figure 2.  The Formation of a New Attitude.

sight—results: the new insight can become the thesis of an essay the writer has been trying to bring into focus. The entire process of sense images' interacting with previously existing configurations, however, is so highly complex that the new insight may not resemble any of its parts. The mind seems not to have gone through a step-by-step process or moved methodically from one point to the next; it has seemingly taken a sudden leap ahead. A writer may say that an "inspiration" suddenly "hit" him. But someone who can write consistently, without having to wait for "inspiration" to "hit" him, has learned to make a conscious effort to fling new sense images into the old configurations that seem most likely to receive them and so bring on the chain reactions that result in new insights—and theses.

*Searching for a thesis.* Assume for the sake of another example that Tom Wolfe [3] went to the Teen Fair in California not with a thesis fully in mind but to look until he saw in the activities an attempt to fulfill universal human needs. As he watched, his sense impressions of hair, shirts, trousers, guitar music, and movements of the dancers joined his understanding of *cool,* and together they sped in his mind among the already-established configurations until they hit the configuration of *form* and merged with it. The now-enhanced configuration, indicating that the activities represented a search for form, was drawn to those configurations representing Versailles and St. Mark's Square and merged with them. The powerful new grouping pulled to it the English Regency configuration and the one representing Europe's "great formal century." The chain reaction completed itself as the sense impressions of the customized cars moved into place and became the symbol of the whole *teen-formal* way of life developing in California. Mr. Wolfe had his insight. His thesis followed: "The 'wild' California teen culture is actually highly formal."

Figure 3 gives a static symbolic representation of how Mr. Wolfe may have searched for an insight that would lead to a thesis. In the flat arrangement of circles, the thesis occupies the inner circle, the previously constructed configurations Mr. Wolfe recalled are shown as small circles within the second circle, and the direct observations he made at the Teen Fair extend along the periphery of the outer circle. For a better, although still static, view of the process, imagine the circle arrangement expanded to form a sphere. Mr. Wolfe's observations on the periphery of the diagram then become more widely spaced about the entire surface of the imaginary

3 See p. 26.

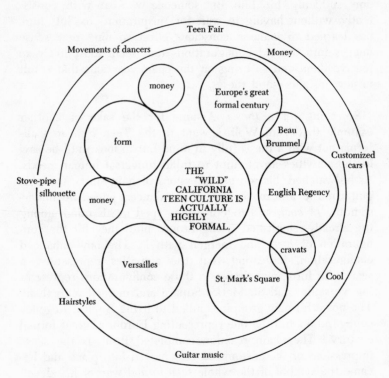

Outer circle ... Direct observations at the Teen Fair
Small circles within the second circle ... Previously constructed meaning configurations
Center circle ... Tom Wolfe's thesis

Figure 3.   New Experience and Previously Acquired Knowledge Interacting to Form the Thesis of Tom Wolfe's Paragraph on the Teen Fair.

sphere. The spherical concept has the advantage of showing the completed insight as a rounded thing, with the beginning found in the end and the end in the beginning.

Figure 4 is an approximation of how one sense impression —movements of the dancers—coming into Tom Wolfe's mind may have reacted with his already existing configurations of form and style (both previously connected with money) and contributed to the new configuration of a formal teen culture.

The spherical configuration is probably the best way to illustrate how insight develops from the reaction between multitudinous sense impressions and the configurations of already existing knowledge. The spherical interpretation seems appropriate to the three-dimensional ideas you work with as a writer.

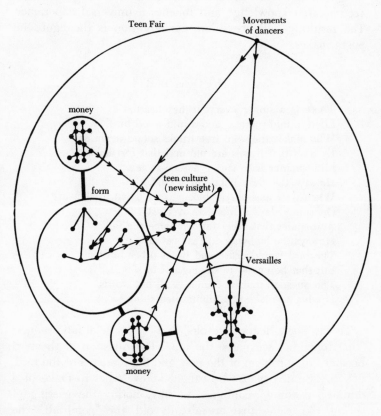

> ———→ Movement of new impression into previously established configurations
> • Elements of previously established configurations
> ▬ Connections between previously established configurations
> →→→ Elements of previously established configurations moving to establish new insight

Figure 4.   The Formation of a New Insight.

*Extending the experience full circle.* The good story, poem, or essay—any finished piece of work—has a kind of roundness to it, too. Robert Frost says, "The figure a poem makes . . . begins in delight and ends in wisdom." He explains, "It has an outcome that . . . was predestined from the first image. . . ." [4] In a number of poems he begins with a concrete delight–image and extends that image until it merges with his accumulated knowledge and touches a universal experience. The resulting delight-wisdom configuration is the figure his poem makes.

### The Oven Bird

> There is a singer everyone has heard,
> Loud, a mid-summer and a mid-wood bird,
> Who makes the solid tree trunks sound again.
> He says that leaves are old and that for flowers
> Mid-summer is to spring as one to ten.
> He says the early petal-fall is past
> When pear and cherry bloom went down in showers
> On sunny days a moment overcast;
> And comes that other fall we name the fall.
> He says the highway dust is over all.
> The bird would cease and be as other birds
> But that he knows in singing not to sing.
> The question that he frames in all but words
> Is what to make of a diminished thing. [5]

To the poet, "leaves are old" and "early petal-fall" suggest "that other fall we name the fall." The question of the bird becomes the problem of the poet and the reader. For the bird, not in joy but because he cannot know "what to make of a diminished thing," continues to sing, noting the passing of spring, the leaves that are already old, the "petal-fall," the "highway dust . . . over all." Almost without the reader's

[4] Robert Frost, "The Figure a Poem Makes," preface, *Complete Poems of Robert Frost* (New York: Holt, Rinehart and Winston, 1964), p. vi.
[5] Robert Frost, "The Oven Bird," from *Complete Poems of Robert Frost* (New York: Holt, Rinehart and Winston, 1964), p. 150. Copyright 1916 by Holt, Rinehart and Winston, Inc. Copyright 1944 by Robert Frost. Reprinted by permission of the publisher.

noticing it, the seasons have been transformed into life and death. Neither bird nor poet can make acceptable the awful truth that living diminishes life. But they can state it and go on living.

The poem, itself an insight, implies a question that explodes into universal possibilities. The poet moves from delight (in the presence of the midsummer bird) to wisdom. The poem comes full circle.

This totality of effect is what all craftsmen, all artists, all composers strive for in their work; it is what the writer strives for in an essay. The essay should give both writer and reader the feeling that the writer has developed his thesis in depth, completed his theme, and said what he intended to say.

### WRITER'S MIND TO PAPER TO READER'S MIND

After the writer has evolved his thesis, he must next compress the three-dimensional configuration in his mind into a linear pattern of words on a flat page—a pattern which should convey to the reader the same meaning it has for the writer. Since, too, the writer's meaning may in his mind be only partially verbal, since it may include associated spheres of pure sensation (sound, smell, taste, feeling, sight), it must be translated—segmented—into the definite intellective utterances called words, and these arranged in precise sequences on paper. Fortunately for both writer and reader, an accurate pattern on the printed page expands in the mind of the reader to the intended configuration—the total *knowing*. Thus the writer's thesis becomes equally "three-dimensional" in the mind of the reader, though transmitted there under imposed limitations of linearity and flatness. This expansion is possible because human experience is universal, because statements can be repeatedly modified until they gain depth and roundness, and because words themselves have two special properties, denotation and connotation.

*Denotation—intellective.* Denotation is the dictionary definition of a word. A word denotes some thing (or concept, quality, condition, etc.)—it means that; it signifies that; it sends that precise signal to the intellect, and the intellect can receive and register the meaning accurately.

The word *flat,* for example, when used to describe a quality of surface, has inescapable meaning to English-speaking people. Two things described as flat may vary in degrees of flatness; a pool table is flat, and a prairie is flat. The concept of flatness remains.

What does *roundness* signify? The roundness of an orange? a baseball? a steel ball bearing? Everyone accepts the concept even though the roundness of the orange is not the precise roundness of a steel ball bearing used in a delicate machine.

What does *wet* mean? Does the expression "It's a wet night" mean that the night is damp and drizzly? beset by passing showers? drenched by a violent rainstorm? The difference is one of degree. The concept of wetness remains.

Even though a single word may have multiple denotations, each of them is fairly definite and relatively fixed. (Note, for example, how many distinctly separate definitions your dictionary lists for the word *down.*)

*Connotation—emotive.* Connotation, on the other hand, is a special sort of atmosphere around some words. It is emotive rather than intellective, felt by the senses rather than understood by the mind. Connotation is the effect of a word's working experience, the sum or average of the associations it has accumulated. For example, the word *home* denotes a dwelling place, but at the same time it connotes warmth, safety, comfort, security, and love. These connotations are generally accepted, generally felt. Even those people whose particular homes may be cold, unsafe, uncomfortable, insecure, or filled with hate, or squalid, or dangerous concede the "good" atmosphere of this word when they encounter it. When they use the word, they assume it will have the standard "atmospheric" effect on their readers or listeners. Consciously or unconsciously they set aside any unusual private associations, and they assume or they hope their readers or listeners will, too. General and special connotations usually overlap, but in cases where they don't, they can coexist peacefully. See Figure 5.

If your reader is to re-create in his mind the mental configurations which you have translated into words, then those words must be precise in denotation and appropriate in connotation. An effective writer is respectful of denotation and sensitive to connotations. He may be said to have developed a "feel for words." It might better be called awareness.

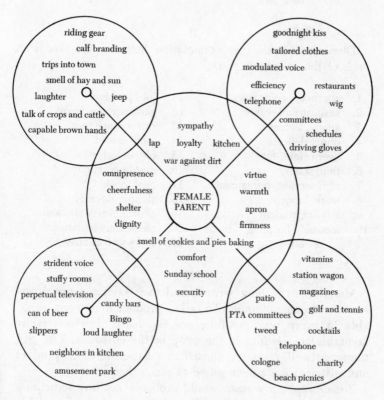

Figures 5.  Overlapping of General and Special Connotations.

## Auxiliary Experiments

### I

In the following sentences, point out the inappropriate words. Discuss their connotations.

1. Mahatma Gandhi's noble example spawned a host of followers.

2. To hide his real identity when he sent a poem to the school magazine, Joe resorted to an alias.
3. My party's platform is concocted of the best that my machine cohorts can muster.
4. On a platter in the middle of the table was the corpse of a hen.

## II

Discuss differences in connotation between the words in each of the following pairs:

1. apathetic, complacent
2. scab, strikebreaker
3. annoy, bother
4. puny, delicate
5. overweight, fat
6. thin, skinny
7. civil servant, bureaucrat
8. work, labor
9. scholar, student
10. mental hospital, insane asylum
11. job, position
12. gardener, yard man
13. disturbance, riot
14. mob, crowd
15. old, elderly
16. customer, client
17. chef, cook
18. sloppy, slovenly
19. poor, poverty-stricken
20. clean, immaculate
21. awkward, clumsy

## III

Manufacturers, their writers, and their salesmen are supersensitive to connotations. To sell, a product must seem desirable in every way possible, not the least of which is by favorable associations in the mind of the customer. The customer, as well, must see himself in a flattering light: product and customer must seem suited to each other.

For example, a woman would probably not buy something called a "sweat stopper" while antiperspirants are available to give her the same effect. Both customer and seller are, incidentally, less fastidious linguistically than the Victorians, who made the distinction that horses sweat, men perspire, and ladies glow—if they mentioned the subject at all.

The same woman is willing to smear her face with cream or, for an extra two or three dollars a jar, with the Frenchified crème. (Anything French in cosmetics or fashion has connotations of exclusiveness, elegance, a charming worldly frivolity, and consummate and irresistible femininity.) The word *smear* is, of course, inappropriate to the entrancing creature the customer must see herself as *almost* being. (With a little help from the product she can *be* that creature—she can fulfill her destiny.) And so the noun *cream* has of necessity become a verb: she can "cream" her face—unless the advertiser decides that her "thirsty" skin needs "feeding." To describe the substances intended for lubricating the human female's skin, the words *grease* and *fat* are as accurate in denotation as *cream* (or *crème*) and *oils* (usually preferable to the singular, and always "blended," not "mixed"). Yet no advertiser has dared to test whether the customer would willingly grease her face with fat.

1. Examine five advertisements of products which would be purchased by or for men. Note the rugged, "masculine" connotations not only of key terms but, in their context, of lesser words, which thus serve as reinforcement. Identify the associations and point out the words which call them up. Look for such concepts as the beast, the hunter, the king, the pasha, the conqueror, and dominance, wildness, strength, bulk, lankiness, leanness.

2. Transform the effect of any heavily connotative advertisement by replacing the key terms and as many as possible of the reinforcing words with words of different connotations but the same denotations.

3. Analyze the connotations of any ten product names. Relate the associations to the customer's needs. For example:

> Ajax—household cleaning agents. Ajax was the mightiest warrior (in terms of brute strength, at least) in the Greek army which demolished Troy. (Achilles was the greatest warrior, all in all, but his name has unfortunate connotations of vulnerability because the expression "Achilles' heel" is in rather common usage.) Ajax the Cleanser, Ajax the Detergent, makes war on dirt. Dirt and therefore household chores will seem puny enemies to the housewife on whose side Ajax is fighting.
>
> Pard—a dog food. A dog is your best friend; your best friend is your comrade, your partner. "Pardner" is a simple, rugged American-cowboy rendition of "partner." "Pard," a shortened form, is a good, friendly name for a dog. It is thus a good name for your dog's best friend, his hearty, rugged, trustworthy dog food.

# Deriving Insights from Readily Available Sources

## USING AN ANTHOLOGY AS SPRINGBOARD

Any anthology of literature is a great source of ideas for subject-man-universal combinations to get you started on an essay. For example, you can think of a poem, or a part of it, in relation to its own time, to its poet, to yourself, to an aspect of the present. If the poem is "ahead of its time," and much great poetry, incidentally, is (even though it might also be called "timeless"), you can consider its poet as misfit, maverick, messiah, social or cultural critic or prophet; you can thus contrast it or him (or it as it reflects his ideas) with its "time": background, milieu, conditions, attitudes, culture, what-have-you.

*Examining a writer in the context of his society.* For example, there is Emerson telling a materialistic, industrializing, westward-pushing people, wasteful and destructive of their country's resources: "Beauty is its own excuse for being." [6] There is Walt Whitman, celebrating indolence in a society to whose members-in-good-standing work and shrewdness were the only acceptable offerings to the god of free enterprise. There is T. S. Eliot, calling the glittering, populous world *The Waste Land,* calling its rushing people "The Hollow Men." Any anthology has dozens of ready contrasts such as these which you can develop from your own knowledge and experience, without research.

If, for example, you are leafing through an anthology of American literature, you might come upon Walt Whitman's "Song of Myself" and read its fourth and fifth lines:

> I loafe and invite my soul,
> I lean and loafe at my ease observing a spear of summer grass. [7]

---

[6] Ralph Waldo Emerson, "The Rhodora."
[7] Walt Whitman, "Song of Myself."

You might be intrigued by the contrast between Whitman's desire to lean and "loafe" as a means of approaching the mystical experience and the desire of other American writers to show that leaning and loafing were short cuts to the poorhouse and the prison. You remember Longfellow's village blacksmith, who was either sweating at his forge or listening to the church choir. You remember Benjamin Franklin's admonition to the youth of America: "Lose no time; be always employed in something useful; cut off all unnecessary actions." And then you remember some of the proverbs that crowded the pages of his *Poor Richard's Almanac*: "Sloth makes all things difficult, but Industry all easy"; "Laziness travels so slowly that Poverty soon overtakes him"; "Let us then be up and doing, and doing to the purpose"; "God gives all things to Industry"; "Plough deep while sluggards sleep"; "Be ashamed to catch yourself idle."

At this point memories of your own experiences move forward. You recall the family lecture your father delivered when he discovered that you and your brother had refused a job mowing a neighbor's lawn because the weather was right for swimming. You remember playing hooky one warm spring afternoon when you were tired of seventh-grade geography; the banquet honoring your grandfather on his retirement after forty-five years with the same company, the gold watch he received—and his death six months later; the fourth-, fifth-, and sixth-grade stories of the Pilgrim Fathers, who took no time for anything but work and worship; your senior term paper on the influence of John Calvin in America; the Puritan idea that work brings signs of God's favor; the conversation you had with hippies in the park last summer; the negligent attitudes of some of the long-haired boys on campus; the songs of Joan Baez, Arlo Guthrie, and Bob Dylan; a television documentary on poverty in the U.S.A.

Again you turn to "Song of Myself." You read the lines

> From the cinder-strew'd threshold I follow their movements,
> The lithe sheer of their waists plays even with their massive
>   arms,
> Overhand the hammers swing, overhand so slow, overhand so
>   sure,

> They do not hasten, each man hits in his place.[8]

and

> The negro that drives the long dray of the stone-yard, steady
>    and tall he stands pois'd on one leg on the string-piece,
> His blue shirt exposes his ample neck and breast and loosens
>    over his hip-band
> His glance is calm and commanding, he tosses the slouch of
>    his hat away from his forehead,
> The sun falls on his crispy hair and mustache, falls on the
>    black of his polish'd and perfect limbs.[9]

You note Whitman's admiration of man for what he is rather
than for his efficiency in producing material things. Perhaps
more importantly, you become aware that Whitman admires
not the work but the natural grace and fulfillment of man
in the act of doing what he has chosen to do, whether it is
hunting, fishing, driving a team, building a home, or merely
singing his joy of life as he tramps the woods and fields. You
note Whitman's appreciation of all experience, his willingness
to allow it. He admires animals because

> Not one is dissatisfied, not one is demented with the mania of
>    owning things.[10]

He admires women who fulfill their function, motherhood:

> I am the poet of the woman the same as the man,
> And I say it is as great to be a woman as to be a man,
> And I say there is nothing greater than the mother of men.[11]

He makes no distinctions between the educated and the un-
educated. He loves men and women because they are human
beings and therefore have human dignity.

Because you are now reading the poem with a purpose,
you become aware that "Song of Myself" presents a broad

[8] *Ibid.*, lines 221-224.
[9] *Ibid.*, lines 226-229.
[10] *Ibid.*, line 689.
[11] *Ibid.*, lines 425-427.

spectrum of Walt Whitman's attitudes. You know that in an essay you cannot be concerned with more than a small part of this spectrum, that you must focus upon one of these attitudes if you are to discover a thesis which you can develop in some detail. You choose his attitude toward leisure, that attitude which first struck you in lines four and five because of its strong contrast with the American tradition of work. You run Walt Whitman's idea through the just-recalled experience configurations in your mind.

The materials you are concentrating upon might be expressed by Figure 6. They could reasonably be expected to evolve in the thesis in the center of the diagram, "Many Americans dislike Walt Whitman because his poetry flouts the American tradition of hard work."

### Long-Haired Loafer

When Walt Whitman published "Song of Myself" in 1855, he expected immediate acclaim. He should have known better.

He should have known even as he began to write the poem that what he was saying was in direct opposition to American traditions and mores. He must have known when he wrote, for example, lines four and five—practically the beginning of the poem—that he was writing defiance, or a confession of treason or of heresy:

> I loafe and invite my soul,
> I lean and loafe at my ease observing a spear of summer
>   grass.

For loafing has no place in the American Way. Nor does "observing a spear of summer grass." The only decent American with any business observing a spear of grass is the scientist, or perhaps the farmer, checking the condition of his pasture. In America an idle mind is the devil's workshop, no place to invite the soul. The American Way is work. The people are committed to it.

But why? Do Americans work simply because they like working? There must be a better reason. To few people is working its own reward. Working cannot be the reward for living; working must produce rewards, something to live for. Working produces things, substance; amasses wealth; provides support for the hard workers in their old age, if they live that

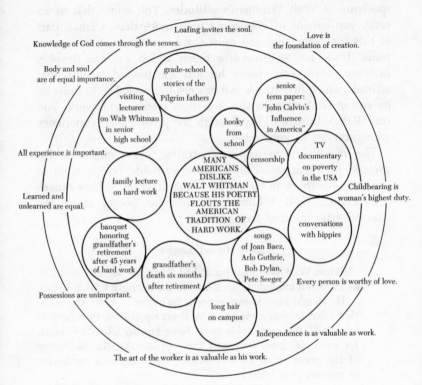

Outer circle . . . Walt Whitman's ideas from "Song of Myself"
Small circles within the second circle . . . Student's previously acquired meaning configurations
Center circle . . . Thesis for composition

**Figure 6.** New Experience and Previously Acquired Knowledge Interacting to Form the Thesis of "Long-Haired Loafer."

long; buys granite monuments. But are these the American Dream, the reason for the American Way? In flouting work and therefore its rewards, did Whitman flout the American Dream? Does American life have no other purpose than *things?*

American life did have, in the beginning.

Amassing wealth may have been the dream of those that came to plunder, but it was not the dream of those that came to work, those that influenced, even established, the American code of values. Material gain was not the aim of an expedition financed by the sweat of journeymen, tradesmen, and farmers, paid for with loneliness and separation, sickness and death on the cold sea and on strange soil. The Pilgrim Fathers, the Puritans, did not dedicate such suffering and sacrifice to amassing things torn up, dug, spaded, chopped, lifted, cut, pulled, gleaned from the rocky soil. They did not come for gain.

Nor did they come for tranquillity, happiness, comfort, or security. They could have had these by staying in England or Holland. These they could have had quite easily, if they had been willing not to be themselves, if they had been willing to pay with their freedom and therefore their peace of mind. They came here to follow what they believed was the will of God.

They sacrificed so much to be free to find peace, a private peace, perhaps to the modern mind a selfish peace. This was the peace of soul that came from the belief (that some of them called knowledge) that they had been chosen and were ruled by God, who had predestined them from all eternity to stand before His throne forever.

At least, they were quite sure He had predestined them. No one could have absolute, positive knowledge, of course, until he died and found out just where he stood. But they saw evidence of God's favor or disfavor in whether their labor bore fruit.

Since they loathed their instincts and distrusted their senses, they could not relax and welcome the mystic, sensual assurance that Walt Whitman would have:

> Swiftly arose and spread around me the peace and
>     knowledge that pass all the argument of the earth,
> And I know that the hand of God is the promise of my
>     own. . . . (lines 91-92)

Walt Whitman ignored (for he must have known) the need for work. But he could relax with *his* God; he could loaf. The two of them were very tolerant, very democratic.

The Puritans' God was another matter entirely. This God was stern, and He was demanding, even of those He had not foreordained to Heaven. And He demanded work.

So the Puritans put their shoulders to the wheel, the seasonal wheel of plowing, planting, cultivating, and reaping. They bound themselves to the plow, the hoe, the scythe, the saw, the sledge, the wedge. Gradually things accumulated: chairs, tables, chests, bedsteads filled cabins larger, warmer, lighter than those that housed the few possessions and the sick, shivering people in the first winters. The cleared fields expanded, cows and sheep dotted the land, and ducks and geese quacked, hissed, and grew fat. Such success could only mean salvation.

But it was work. Long labor under the hot sun made the faint of heart or body lean against the half-burned stumps in the clearings, lean and loaf to catch their breath—and wonder why. Gradually those who could not take the labor, along with the loafers for whom the bright vision had faded, drifted into want or, landless, wifeless, moved into the wilderness with rifle and trap, to be pointed out or remembered as those God had rejected, had damned before they were born.

The work that brought an accumulation of earthly things that indicated God's chosen among His creatures contrasted strongly with the improvidence, shiftlessness, and poverty that marked God's rejected ones. This contrast, strengthened by example after example, passed from father to son to son and became the American judgment, the acceptable—the obvious—means of separating good from evil.

The stream of school teachers that flowed from Harvard College and spread across the land washed the minds of generations of children with this Puritan heritage, this middle-class ethic: Work and Succeed (work and gain; work and lay up treasure). That the gain, the success, and the treasure were only signs of God's approval, not ends in themselves, mattered less as time went on. The stern God shared his throne now with a golden calf.

Only a fool would defy such a coalition. Poor Walt Whitman! How ridiculous an American, leaning on his elbow and singing of bathing in the forest pools. No wonder he was fired from his job in Washington—he did everything wrong.

Even when he admired the laborers, he admired them for the wrong reason. He said nothing about how much they accomplished. He loved the way teamsters lounged atop the loaded drays and the negligent way they handled the double teams.

He admired mothers because they were fecund, not because they were skilled at washing, scrubbing, cooking, or sewing. There was something unholy about Whitman's attitude toward women. It signaled for a return to the worship of the mythic goddesses in man's unconscious memories.

His poetry outraged clergymen, who shouted, "Blasphemy!" and "He believes in free love!" It shocked critics, who screamed about the sensibilities of cultivated man, offended by this unrhymed, unmusical voice. (They agreed with Whitman only when he termed his poetry a "barbaric yawp over the roofs of the world" [line 1333].)

But Whitman, damned and dangerous, the true imperturbable one, answered not a word. He knew that loafing is as much a part of man as working is. He saw man as a part of nature and his natural actions as honesty. He knew that man has a responsibility to be himself that cannot be ignored or whipped into conformity with unnatural custom. He knew that a man who was truly himself would go beyond indifference and tolerance and find unselfish love. He knew "that a kelson of the creation is love" (line 95). Long-haired, long-bearded loafer, lover of mankind, no wonder he offended almost everyone.

He still does.

## Auxiliary Experiments

### I

The following refer to Figure 6 and the essay "Long-Haired Loafer."

1. Point out the contrasts between Whitman's ideas (outer circle) and those experience configurations (inner circles) having to do with "establishment" ideas.

2. How do the contrasts function to effect the formulation of thesis?

3. Point out likenesses between Whitman's ideas and the ideas expressed in some of the inner circles.

4. How do the likenesses function to effect the formulation of thesis?

5. Discuss the possibility that conflicting ideas set up tensions that force a writer to make up his mind and so formulate a thesis.

6. In the mind of the writer of "Long-Haired Loafer," what inner-circle configurations may have combined to give rise to the following concepts?

a. "The American Way"
b. The equation of work with goodness

## II

Choose any experience of yours. By constructing a diagram similar to Figure 5, arrive at a thesis.

*Recognizing yourself in the words of others.* Any book has dozens of ready ideas which can serve as springboards, as points of departure, for your own ideas, thoughts, or attitudes about anything within your actual or vicarious experience. Any anthology is an especially good source because the ideas and the point of view will vary and shift from author to author. But the poetry anthology is probably best of all. Ideas vary from poem to poem, and, because poetry is by its nature more intense, more "packed" than prose, they occur with greater frequency and in a wider range of nuances.

*In leafing through a book of poetry and looking for ideas for essays, remember that you are not now studying literature or reading for enjoyment, not looking for information or even for impressions utterly new to you. You are looking through the common experiences of men for a comment you yourself can make.*

Certainly the gorgeous urgency of Marvell's "Had we but world enough, and time. . . ." [12] has been felt and insisted on, in and out of paraphrase, millions of times since the seventeenth century, even as the universal urge the line captures had been felt and insisted on for thousands of years before. Think of how the same idea echoes flippantly in Herrick's "Gather ye rosebuds while ye may. . . ." [13] Do you recognize anything of yourself in John Donne's "I wonder, by my troth, what thou and I/Did, till we loved?" [14] Skip ahead a few centuries in literature and back a few years in your life. Do you recognize the wild, surging feelings of your own adolescence in Dylan Thomas's "The force that through the green fuse drives the flower/Drives my green age. . . ."? [15]

[12] Andrew Marvell, "To His Coy Mistress."
[13] Robert Herrick, "To the Virgins, To Make Much of Time."
[14] John Donne, "The Good Morrow."
[15] Dylan Thomas, "The Force That Through the Green Fuse Drives the Flower."

Alert to the universals reflected in the poems, you are really searching through your own experiences, knowledge, and old sense impressions; you are searching for something already there in your own memory, poking at your memory to rouse out of it those things which you can put together and share with a reader.

For example, when you read Cummings' lines "how do you like your blueeyed boy/Mister Death," [16] free your mind of Buffalo Bill. Think of *boy* and *death*. Is there a connection between the two ideas in your own experience? Think of a boy dead, any boy. Boys should not die. Death is for the old. Boys are for life. The boy dead. Murder? Suicide? Highway accident? War? A child's body in the rubble of a bombing? A soldier, not much more than a boy, dead in a war he didn't start? Let your thoughts form images, and let these call up other thoughts, and knowledge, and memories of thoughts and experiences. Let ideas come. You have much to say, much to write.

### Auxiliary Experiment

Try the above-described process yourself. Record your associations and ideas. Explore one thesis possibility and construct a diagram similar to Figure 6.

### USING THE INTERVIEW

More subject to control than "constructive eavesdropping," but more demanding, is the interview as a means of finding a viable thesis in an already established object-man-universal relationship. Almost anything that someone owns or uses or does can be the subject of your interview of him; such is the human psyche that almost anyone is willing to talk about what he owns or what he does, if only because he is startled to discover that anyone is interested in him. The interviewer looking for a thesis should direct his questions to the discovery of *why* rather than *how, when, where,* or *who.* Once he has discovered the *why,* he can go beyond the usual journalistic formula and use the results of the interview to trans-

[16] E. E. Cummings, "Buffalo Bill's."

form his original subject, as Tom Wolfe did when he wrote the paragraph about the Teen Fair. Again, as with Mr. Wolfe's experience, the emphasis should be on insights rather than on conclusions.

As an example of how an everyday object can be used to develop a thesis, consider the bucket seat.

At seven-thirty on a Friday evening you notice a young man sitting in his XT 423 at the local drive-in, eating a hamburger and drinking a milkshake. You glance quickly at the radial-ply tires; you hear the stereo tape playing. You walk up to the car just as he stuffs the paper napkin into the empty cup, places it on the tray, and begins to strap himself into the bucket seat.

"Quite a car."
"Yeah."
"Do you like the bucket seat?"

As he tightens the seat belt and shoulder harness, you are reminded of the Mexican Indians of ever so long ago who thought at first that the mounted Spaniards were a new kind of animal, six-legged, two-headed—fused together by some unknown god.

"It wraps me up, man. I don't slide around in it."
"Why would you slide around?"

The bucket seat gives the driver security and protection.

"When you weave in and out with this thing, the G's work on you, fast. This car is a real tiger, a real big cat. When I say 'Jump,' it jumps."
"A real tiger, eh?"

The comparison to the tiger exemplifies man's desire to exercise complete mastery over those elements that might otherwise kill him.

"Yeah. A tiger in a cage— and I got the whip."

The driver insists upon complete control of the powerful machine.

"You're the boss?"
"It does what I want it to do."
"Such as?"
"When I want it to cut, it cuts. Those radials bite right in."

The response of this car gives him a feeling of personal accomplishment.

"How does it feel?"

"Great."

"But what does it feel like?"

"It feels like I'm riding it. All of me and all of it get together."

The bucket seat gives the driver the feeling that he and the machine are one unit.

"Like a motorcycle?"

"Yeah. Lots of horses under me. And nobody telling me what to do. I'm the boss. I just rev and move out."

The motorcycle image and then that of the horse give the impression that the driver is urged by a primitive desire to feel power and to control that power completely.

"Do you like to drive it alone?"

"I'm always alone once it's moving. No one else in the car counts. A 423 and four on the floor ain't for sharing."

Is this a need for privacy?

"Do you like to do things all by yourself?"

"A man has to do something all by himself. What I mean is, be free to do some things all by himself."

The driver resents being told what to do. He wants to have some area within which he can realize himself as a man.

"Can't you do other things all by yourself?"

"Nothing that counts."

"What do you do on the job?"

"Make casting molds."

"Are you good at it?"

"Better than most."

"Do you get a kick out of it?"

"I licked that job long ago."

Do mechanization and automation deny man the opportunity to express himself through work?

"Do you like your job?"

"It's money."

"That's all?"

"The other sixteen hours are mine."

The driver shows clearly that his job is only a means to an end. With the money he earns he buys the one thing over which he can exercise complete control.

He turns the key. The glasspacks roar. His head cocked to listen, he hardly notices the car hop as she hurriedly picks up the tray. Evidently satisfied with the sound, he nods to you. The interview is over. You watch him drive away.

You may have noticed that not all the reactions and reflections noted in the right-hand column above concern the bucket seat even indirectly. You may also have noticed that those which tend to be interpretive are based more on your old knowledge than on the interview. The essay that grows out of these may well concern itself with any number of subjects suggested by the interview but based on your other accumulated experience.

In searching for insights from which to develop a thesis, you might reasonably ask yourself this question: Why does this young man feel there is little or nothing he can do "that counts"? What is there in his environment to make him feel so curtailed and limited as a human being that he turns to a car for self-expression?

In a personal struggle with a powerful machine, a machine designed to lose this "struggle" (if the opponent is expert) and be mastered, constructed to obey within defined limits the whims of its operator, this man finds expression but also, in winning, satisfaction and even fulfillment. In his mastery of this machine he finds a satisfaction that he can not easily find elsewhere in his life. His work, which ideally should challenge and satisfy him, is probably useless as an outlet for his desire to dominate some part of his environment. The performance of his job, long since "licked," he has reduced to habit; he can do his work automatically. On the job, he is himself a machine.

If he is to feel like a man, he needs to remind himself that he is a man. He needs constantly to prove himself to himself.[17] Because he is civilized, he does not inflict his will on other men, forcing proof from them. Because he is adult, he does not ask them for reassurance. (You recall that nowhere in the interview did the young man mention that the sport car impressed his friends or his enemies or the general public.) As the concept of the car reverts metaphorically to that of a motorcycle and then a horse, the young man becomes every

[17] Elaboration on this universal theme made Ernest Hemingway famous.

man urged by a primitive part of his nature to dominate other creatures, to make them feel the force of his will. If that mastery cannot be found in the ordinary affairs of life, if there are no opportunities to exert a personal control, he will work to simulate such a world. Because this urge is primitive and private, he needs to be alone during his working-out of symbolic victories over the machine.

In a sense, perhaps, these are also victories over his other self, that self which is a machine. By extension, these can be considered subconscious struggles between the independent, self-determining, assertive self and the un-willing creature of habit, the automaton, the slave, that self less than a man, that mere car, that beast. These struggles and victories are profoundly personal. The young man needs to be alone during them, apart from society (even if only symbolically), insulated from all others, neither helped nor hindered by his fellow men.

The bucket seat provides that insulation and, with its seat belt and shoulder strap to bind him closely, gives him the feeling of unity with that which he dominates. When he masters the car, its power becomes his power, his stature increases, and his image of himself is enhanced. He is someone. He knows he *is*.

Thus through this one young man, briefly encountered in the drive-in lot, you have gained access to old knowledge, knowledge of yourself and of others, accumulated through the million human encounters of your life. Through him you have discovered in your memory that which needed only this insight and the consciousness of it and then the deliberate use of it to be made worthwhile. For your purposes, this young man is more than one particular person because he shares with countless other particular persons one of countless universal human needs. He is every man; in him your reader can see himself.

## Auxiliary Experiments

1. Conduct your own interview. From the insights you gain, work out at least two theses suitable for five-hundred-word development. The following suggestions may help.

People with hobbies or avocations:
    Motorcyclist
    Driver of any unusual vehicle
    Rose gardener
    Renaissance coffeehouse manager
    Photographer
    Painter or sculptor
    Ceramicist
    Weaver
    Civil War buff
    Railroad buff
    Steam-automobile restorer
    Astronomer
    Sky diver
    Occultist

People in action:
    Picketer—for any reason
    Demonstrator
    Instructor in any skill—judo, karate, fencing
    Go-go dancer
    Black militant
    Transcontinental truck driver
    Ambulance driver
    Bookie
    Fireman
    VISTA worker
    Public-health nurse
    Real-estate salesman

People making purchase decisions:
    At the gourmet shop or department
    At the wine store or department:
            Connoisseur
            Hesitant housewife
            Old wino
            Self-styled man-of-the-world
    At the antique auction:
            Dealer
            Collector
            Curiosity seeker and sometime purchaser of "bargains"
    At the flea market
    At the magic store
    At the health-food counter or store

2. As a rather difficult exercise in gaining insight, interview yourself. Limit the interview to one aspect of your life, preferably one you feel either makes you part of a group or brings you into conflict with a group. Draw up at least one thesis for five-hundred-word development. In it refer to yourself not as "I" but according to the role you play in that part of your life the interview concentrates on—for example, haunter of coffeehouses, pursuer of causes, member of _____, lover of _____, hater of _____.

## STARTING FROM UNIVERSALS

In looking for ideas to develop into theses for essays, you can also start with the universal—say love, or hate—and think of manifestations, or instances, of it. Any manifestation of a universal involves man.

*Narrowing the too-broad subject.* Denis de Rougemont wrote a 336-page book entitled *Love in the Western World.* But this is only its title. Its subject is courtly love. Its thesis is that courtly love, a phenomenon resulting from a complex combination of circumstances and conditions, has profoundly influenced Western literature, manners, morals, and thus culture, even history. There are hundreds of aspects of love the book does not treat because De Rougemont did not choose to treat them and therefore did not imply them in his thesis. He did not want to write an encyclopedia of love. He wanted to examine a single phenomenon thoroughly; he wanted to develop a thesis. The hundreds of other aspects are extraneous to courtly love as a phenomenon; they are unrelated to his thesis; they would be superfluous to his development of it; they would only pad his book.

It is necessary to control the impulse to treat a universal as a subject. If you were to set yourself the task of writing about love (or hate, or generosity, or cowardice) in a five-hundred-word or a thousand-word essay, then you would be naïve indeed—if not about the subject itself, then certainly about writing. On so broad a subject, you could say only general things—generalities, either obvious or vague. In trying to cover such a subject you would merely cover space—with platitudes, probably. It would be a very thin cover; it would be a very shallow treatment. You would realize something was wrong; you would feel frustrated because you could not get down to cases, be relevant to anything meaningful, say anything to change anyone's mind, make anything clearer to anyone than it had been before. If you tried to be specific, your treatment could be only a scattering of bird shot over a vast target. Your reader, if he stayed with you long enough to read all five hundred or one thousand words, would learn only that you are in favor of love or against hate, that you like generosity or disapprove of cowardice. Although he would quite probably share your attitude, he would find no value in your essay. It would waste his time. What everybody agrees on need hardly be reiterated.

*Reversing the subject-man-universal approach.* So you get down to cases *before* you begin the essay. You work from the universal to particular manifestations of it to arrive at a thesis. You think, or imagine, or project toward the concrete —on paper, first of all in a list.

This procedure will have a rather strong relationship to the stream-of-consciousness technique you used when you got your own ideas from a newspaper article (p. 46), with the difference that you now exercise a certain control—set limits to the wandering you encourage your mind to do.

Jot down in a single list whatever you associate with one universal, with, say, the word *love*. At this stage, do not distract yourself by considering the essay you will eventually write. Jot down the associations consecutively as they occur, even though you realize that one is closely related to or part of an earlier one. To stop and go back, to try now to arrange the items in the list, would distract you, too, and slow or curtail the process.

Almost all the items in your list will be more specific than the word you are working with. It is with those that are equally general, or nearly so, that you must be a bit careful. Here control is necessary. For example, from *love* you might get *peace* and then *war* and then *democracy* or *imperialism* or *weariness* or *death*. Any of these might lead you off on a tangent if you allowed it.

Probably your associations will not arrive neatly in the same grammatical category, nor should they, necessarily. Don't waste time or distract yourself by making them parallel or putting them in agreement. They may be a mixture of adjectives, questions, phrases, statements—anything. It does not matter. This is a working list and usually quite a private one; it is only a means to an end. The following list is the result of ten minutes of controlled association with the word *love*.

Sharing
Hand in hand
No more loneliness
Pets teach children to give love
Flirting
Suffering
Suspense
Self-denial
Silence and warmth
Sex
Romance and sex compatible?
Romance and honesty compatible?
Excitement
Happiness
Pleasure, joy
Dating—artificial custom?
Springtime, June-moon, brides
Marriage
Listening together
Creation
Bodies
Babies
Children playing
Singing
Brotherhood—all men brothers
Hatred—blindness
Bitterness, hurt feelings
Maturity
Working to help someone
Sacrifice
Parenthood
I love my parents; do they know?
Dying
Homesickness, love of a place
Loving your enemies

Understanding
Jealousy
Talking to someone, leveling with—
God is love, loving is prayer
Creation
Black, white, brown, yellow, red
Protecting someone
Tied down, loss of freedom
Selfishness
Playboy philosophy
Romantic poets
Love songs
Elopement
Rescue, melodrama, soap opera
Perpetuate my name

When your list fills the page, or when the associations stop flowing, it is time to read what you have jotted down. It is not yet time to think about an essay. The next step is to extend some of the items into as many meaningful statements, questions, or at least phrases as you can. Each of these will be more definite or particular than the item it developed from (which in turn is more definite or particular than the universal concept *love*). These statements may embody examples of love, or causes, or effects; they will deal with love (the universal) in its manifestations (more or less particular cases, involving man); they will contain or imply subjects, and they will translate more or less easily into theses.

Now go through the list again. Cross off those items which seem too broad or general, those which seem least interesting, and those which for any other reason you could not do justice to in an essay.

Think about the remaining items. Some more than others will appeal to you as a person, or as a writer. They will seem almost willing to be written about, willing to be developed or supported.[18] Ask yourself why they appeal to you, what it is

[18] There may be in this second list a statement which seems to cry to you for defense against its enemies or urge you to campaign on its behalf. If you find such a statement, you almost undoubtedly have not only a ready thesis but the best possible thesis on this subject *for you*, one that you can devote yourself to eagerly and write very strongly on. There is no reason then to look further for a thesis, but the process the following paragraphs describe will help you gather material for your essay on it.

in each that can be brought out, that you can share with a reader in a way that can appeal to him.

Next to each of these few, or several, items jot down whatever you can bring forth from it: detail, backing, insights, examples, causes, effects. You'll no doubt need to lay a second sheet to the right of the first if you're to have space enough. Make these third-stage entries as complete as you can; again, form sentences, questions, or at least phrases. You'll notice that you can expand on one or two of the items much more than the others. (In Figure 7, notice the varying degrees of expansion of the first six associations from the list on page 91. The variation lies with the writer, not with the universal or the associations.) You'll notice, too, that some of the third-stage entries seem to attract to themselves items from the first two columns (including some you have checked off); you'll find yourself drawing lines and arrows to attach them to what has become your major idea. You are gathering material from which you can best develop an essay.

By this time your two pages (taped together, probably, to facilitate your lines and arrows) are very crowded. Stop now, and examine the largest cluster of ideas. Perhaps the second-stage statement that they center on is a ready-made thesis. Perhaps a third-stage item is or can be converted to one. Perhaps several items together express or imply a thesis. Perhaps your thesis is the sum of all the parts of the cluster. Somewhere in this material is your thesis, actual or potential. You will recognize it as your own, and you will realize that much of the remaining material will help you develop it.

Figure 7. Using Free Association To Find Theses and Material for Their Development.

**SHARING**

Doing everything together.
I would like to share something wonderful I'm seeing for the first time, something I like, my thoughts on everything, something I'm reading that I have, the things I remember, what I was like when I was a little kid, the places I like to go, our old neighborhood, my future.
If you love someone, you want to share everything with that person, except bad things—you want to protect her from unhappiness, unpleasantness.
You want to share your friend's or lover's unhappiness, though, so you can make the burden of it less.

**HAND IN HAND**

When you're little, your mother holds your hand to keep you from getting lost in the store, or to cross the street.
As you get older, you think it's a kid thing to hold hands—when you're seven, you'd die of shame if anyone saw you hold your mother's hand.
When you're in junior high and hold a girl's hand, it's like taking a trip. You're flying. But you'd die of shame if someone saw you.
When you're in high school and you hold your steady's hand, it's all right, and the others stay away.
I saw an old couple holding hands. They were beautiful, like kids.
Shaking hands is like holding hands, almost a symbol of holding hands?

**NO MORE LONELINESS**

If two lonely people come together, maybe they can fill each other's emptiness. They find each other and they're not lonely anymore.
If you're in love with someone who loves you, then someone cares if you live or die.
Someone is there, and you don't have to come into an empty place.
If you call, there's an answer.

Would you want to do everything together? What about privacy?
Can married people have privacy?
If love doesn't include respect for privacy, the one loved changes.
Then you don't have the same person and can't love her.
Sometimes you don't share your troubles because you don't want to depress people.
Sometimes you don't share your problems because you don't want somebody to worry.
So too much consideration can slow down communication. If you can't communicate, what kind of relationship is that?
Good manners can kill people. You don't tell someone he's too drunk to drive: "Let me drive; you're not capable."
In Ministry of Fear, the man is too polite to interrupt a seance, so he doesn't say, "I think I'm going to be murdered any minute."

Hand in hand symbolizes trust? equality? helping? warmth?
Holding hands is more real than giving a girl your arm.
Shaking hands is a good old custom, a warm thing to do—it says, "I welcome you into my life, I share a little of my privacy with you, I give you a little of me—tentatively. We are holding hands for size."

Maybe two lonely people find they have only loneliness in common. That's not enough.
Love isn't an escape from the human condition. Nor is sex.
Older generation think so.
"Happily ever after," meant sex? Escape from villain, from loneliness: from human condition—therefore end of story.
They cover sex with veneer of romance, flirtation, bachelor dinners, honeymoons, symbolic rice.
Now emphasis is on sharing, without the stabilizing rituals.
Rituals meant protectively but as likely to lead to unhappiness as to happiness.
Is society concerned with happiness or with protection?

Easter chicks, baby ducks—kids love them and they die, of too much love.

While the kid is learning all this responsibility, the poor animal starves.

Love isn't real love if it doesn't let the one loved be himself. Some love smothers people. Too much love is smothering. Possessiveness.

Some parents. Doting husband—foolish. Doting grandparents—destructive.

Advancing, retreating, feinting. Like boxing? Like shadow-boxing.

Flirtation is a conventionalization—stylized war between the sexes.

Flirtation is a custom. It shouldn't be necessary any more, like offering your arm, as if a girl might trip in her size-8 shoes. Purpose gone.

Dogs and cats suffer. A little kid, a two-year-old, grabs the cat's tail because it's there, and maybe waving. But big kids: a kid tied two tomcats together and they fought until one died. The guys said he was sick. Tomcats like to fight, though, even when there's no female to fight over. An old tom goes out looking for a fight—not happy until he's bloody, his ears are shredded, one eye is closed. Then he staggers home and sleeps till the next night's action. But he can't want to suffer, only to fight.

Somebody who owns a fighting cock loves it, as somebody else loves a dog. Then how can he put it in with another fighting cock and let them try to kill each other? They wouldn't have to fight, but it's in their blood to fight—maybe they love to fight. Maybe the owners are letting them fulfill their destiny, live fully, by encouraging their instincts? They breed them to be brave. The fight and suffering and inflicting of suffering are the climax of a cock's life? The reason he was hatched?

Loving a thing or a person is respecting; let it be what it is. Does that include encouraging it to be itself and get hurt?

Loving can't be control, or it's slave and master, thing and owner.

## PETS TEACH CHILDREN TO GIVE LOVE

Pets are an outlet for love.

Having a pet to take care of builds character, responsibility, etc., in children.

How can anybody love a bird? Birds, yes, singing outside, but if you love a bird, chances are he's captive. Is the kind of person who can love a bird in a cage cruel? selfish? unsure of himself so he has to keep the thing he loves trapped and captive? If he loved the bird as a bird, for itself, wouldn't he let it go? Let it be a bird, be itself? Then it might die, if it's never been free before. Am I anti-bird or anti-keeping-them-in-cages? How can you love something you can't trust?

## FLIRTING

It's artificial; it's imitation love, pretense, hypocrisy.

Maybe it isn't hypocritical if the person being flirted with flirts back and both people know what's going on—each one knows the other is flirting and knows he knows. Then it's a game. Silly game. Practice? Practice for the big game?

But otherwise (maybe anyhow) it's a form of lying.

## SUFFERING

Being in love can be like suffering—is suffering at some stages.

But you wouldn't give up the suffering if it meant not loving whoever or whatever made you suffer.

Willingness to suffer for something or somebody is a sort of test of love or of loyalty to what or who is loved. Christ suffered. Soldiers have always suffered—some of them. Do some soldiers like to inflict suffering?

When little kids tear bugs apart—dismember them—slowly, are they being scientific or are they getting kicks out of causing suffering? The mothers would say the kids love bugs and have scientific curiosity. I think they're probably sadists. But do the bugs really suffer?

Suffering is relative? Maybe what somebody considers suffering isn't suffering for someone else.

Like going to the sauna. Or my cousin—idea of heaven is being wet, half-frozen, tired, hungry, sitting in a boat shooting at ducks.

Some people like to suffer—masochists. Sick.

# CHAPTER FOUR

# Efficiency in the Job of Writing

## The Myth of Mood and Inspiration

[*First Stage*]

Ah time, oh night, oh day
~~Ni nal ni na, na ni~~
~~Ni na ni na, ni na~~
Oh life O death, O time
　Time a di
~~Never Time~~
Ah time, a time O-time
　~~Time!~~

[*Second Stage*]

Oh time, oh night oh day
~~O day oh night, alas~~
　~~O~~ Death time night ~~oh~~
Oh, Time
Oh time o night oh day

[*Third Stage*]

[1]

Na na, na na na' na
Nă nă na na na—nă nă
　Nă nă nă nă nā nā
Na na nā nā nâ ă na

Na na na—nă nă—na na
　Na na na na—na na na na na
Na na na na na.
　　　Na na
Na na na na na
　　　Na na
Na na na na na ă na!

[2]

Oh time, oh night, o day
  alas
 O day ~~serenest,~~ o day
 O day alas the day
That thou shouldst sleep when we awake to say

O time time—o death—o day
 O day, o death for life is far from thee
 O thou wert never free
 For death is now with thee
 ~~And life is far from~~
 O death, o day for life is far from thee


  [*Published Version, 1824*]

O world! O life! O time!
On whose last steps I climb,
 Trembling at that where I had stood before;
When will return the glory of your prime?
  No more—Oh, never more!

Out of the day and night
A joy has taken flight;
 Fresh spring, and summer, and winter hoar,

Move my faint heart with grief, but with delight
  No more—Oh, never more! [1]


Here is Shelley, archetype of inspired poets, working out his
ideas. In the great age of romanticism in which he lived, the
avant-garde believed that the spirit could be found only
through emotion. Yet not the spirit, nor even emotion, would
pour directly onto the page. Good writing did not come automatically even to those poetic geniuses who could hear their
own hearts; who were tuned in to the spirit; who were, some
of them, turned on with the help of opium. It was as it had
been in the eighteenth century, when Richard Sheridan said,

[1] Percy Bysshe Shelley, "The Lament," *The Norton Anthology of
English Literature,* Revised, ed. M. H. Abrams *et al.* (New York: W. W.
Norton & Co., Inc., 1968), II, 722-724. Copyright © 1968, 1962
by W. W. Norton & Co., Inc.

"Easy writing's vile hard reading," [2] and as it still is and has always been. Good writing is invariably work.

William Blake, the mystic, whose inspiration was direct and genuine beyond a doubt, applied the same meticulous craft to his poetry as he did to his marvelous engravings. Byron's quick-witted satire against the establishment was not merely spontaneous; and his long poems of the alienated were long, hard work.

Keats's working drafts are the most famous holographs in the English language. Here is the twenty-fourth stanza of "The Eve of Saint Agnes" in four stages of development:

```
1        A Casement ~~ach'd~~ tripple archd and diamonded
2        With many coloured glass fronted the Moon
                      wereof
3     In midst ~~of which~~ a shilded scutcheon shed
4        High blushing gules ~~upon she kneeled saintly~~ down
5        And inly prayed for grace and heavenly boon
6        The blood red gules fell on her silver cross
7     And ~~her~~ white (est) hands devout


      There was
1        A Casement tipple archd and high
2           All garlanded with carven imageries
3        Of fruits ~~& trailing~~ flowers and sunny corn
                                        ears parchd


1        A Casement high and tripple archd there was
2           All gardneded with carven imageries
3        Of fruits and flowers and bunches of knot grass;
4        And diamonded with panes of quaint device
5        Innumerable of stains and splendid dies
                                    sunset
      As is the tger moths ~~rich~~ deep ~~damasked~~ wings
6     ~~As is the wing of evening tiger moths;~~
            whereft    thousand
7     ~~And~~ in ~~the~~ midst 'mong ~~man~~ heraldries
8        And ~~dim twilight~~ twilight saints and dim emblasonings
9     A shielded scutcheon blushd with Blood of Queens & Kings
```

[2] Richard Brinsley Sheridan, "Clio's Protest," *The Plays and Poems of Richard Brinsley Sheridan,* ed. R. Crompton Rhodes (New York: Russell and Russell, Inc., 1962), III, 117.

| | |
|---|---|
| 1 | A casement high and triple-arched there was, |
| 2 | All garlanded with carven imag'ries |
| 3 | Of fruits, and flowers, and bunches of knot-grass, |
| 4 | And diamonded with panes of quaint device, |
| 5 | Innumerable of stains and splendid dyes, |
| 6 | As are the tiger moth's deep-damasked wings; |
| 7 | And in the midst, 'mong thousand heraldries, |
| 8 | And twilight saints, and dim emblazonings, |
| 9 | A shielded scutcheon blushed with blood of queens and kings.[3] |

It is a myth that a piece of writing is the manifestation of a sort of mystic gift, that can be only received, never sought. The myth arose centuries ago and continued because some writers have always preferred discussing their "gifts" to admitting their hard work, as if there were something rather shameful about craft or skill or labor. They were believed, and the belief seems to renew itself endlessly.

Those who perpetuate the myth, ignoring any evidence to refute it, do so because it is a useful myth; because refusing to believe it would leave no time and no excuse for the peaceful, self-pitying contemplation of blank walls, blank paper, the specter of the blank diploma.

Any writing assignment is a job to do, no more and no less. "Inspiration" may help you get started, but it won't come when you call. The mood to write may help you get on with the job, but it is as capricious as inspiration, and as recalcitrant.

You are given writing assignments. You are asked to be clear, not clever; exact, not exotic. You want to be interesting, whether or not you are asked to be. (As if anyone could want to be dull!) You will have time to make your writing clear and strong and all the rest if you don't waste time waiting for the inspiration, or the mood, which may never come.

---

[3] John Keats, "The Eve of Saint Agnes," *The Norton Anthology of English Literature*, Revised, ed. M. H. Abrams *et al.* (New York: W. W. Norton & Co., Inc., 1968), II, 724. Copyright © 1968, 1962 by W. W. Norton & Co., Inc.

## Working Like a Professional

When good amateurs are playing, some spectators will say, "They're good enough to play professionally." But, when the good amateur plays the professional, the differences between the two are usually apparent. And it is apparent that the amateur can learn from the professional.

So it is with writers.

The professional writer, like the professional sportsman, goes about his work in the way he has found best suited to his own special talents. He plans his work, and he follows through with methods and techniques he has found successful.

### SCHEDULE YOUR WRITING TIME

Most professional writers work according to schedules. They don't work against time; they work within time. Thousands of writers are salaried; they write for six or seven or eight hours a day, five days a week. "Free-lance" writers, who can control their own writing time, do control it. Most of them set themselves strict schedules and follow them. One, for example, may write for four uninterrupted hours each morning or afternoon. At the end of that set period, he stops working on that particular project until the next day. Although schedules are individual matters, they can be definite, and once set they can be adhered to. The process of writing may be a very personal one, but it can be controlled.

To write each assignment, set up at least two blocks of time, separated by a span of hours that includes if possible a night's sleep—for example, two hours on Monday afternoon and two on Tuesday evening. You thus provide yourself with a safety valve for the release of tensions generated by the effort of writing. You provide yourself and the essay a cooling-off period. When you return to the draft and reread it, you can keep a certain aesthetic distance between you and your production. You can see in it weaknesses—and strengths—you overlooked during the first session. You can be objective when you reread the draft, and firm and decisive when you rewrite it. Time will have given you perspective.

## PLAN

You have a thesis. You already have much material to develop it—material you jotted down when you were working toward insights, material you winnowed through to get the thesis. Now you need a plan.

There are rare people in whose heads plans seem to grow unaided, in marvelous detail and perfect order. Among them are even rarer ones in whose heads the plans remain while they carry them out—in marvelous detail and perfect order. Most people, however, without at least rudimentary plans—worked out beforehand and put down on paper, to be held in the hand and consulted from time to time—can only bumble and bungle along, trusting to luck or relying on trial and error and much time to accomplish what they intend. With few exceptions, even brilliant people who have excellent memories draw up plans—for the sake of simplicity and efficiency and the conservation of energy.

Plans hold still while you examine them; they wait unchanging while your mind occupies itself with other considerations, other subjects; they help you to foresee eventualities in their carrying out; they make evident weaknesses and omissions before these can cause serious trouble; they save you time; they save you effort; they may save you embarrassment and disappointment.

A plan is a sketch, a layout, a blueprint, a mockup, a scale model. The plan is like a skeleton, to which, in writing the essay, you carefully attach muscles. For this creature of yours, think of the thesis as brain, controlling all the parts through a nervous system of meaning.

The plan for an essay may be the traditional outline,[4] a mere list, a list made more useful by the addition of lines and arrows, a preliminary summary (a brief expansion of the thesis, which is itself the ultimate summary of the essay), or any of a number of diagrams.

[4] See p. 127.

The most important thing to remember about any plan, be it the most formal sentence outline or the most crudely drawn diagram, is that *it is flexible*. Plans are not rigid, though many people treat them as if they were. You do not "deviate from the plan" if you find at some point you cannot follow it; you simply adjust the plan to the circumstances you did not foresee in making it. You continue with the *revised* plan—you don't abandon the original and wander along, hoping you'll arrive somewhere.

Think of driving some distance, following a route you plotted carefully on a road map before starting. When you come to a detour sign, it would be foolhardy to ignore it and try to cross the river where the bridge has been washed out. It would be equally foolhardy to throw the map away. Doing either would never occur to you. You make the detour, penciling it in on the map. Or you spread out the map and plot a new route for the remainder of the journey.

For long drives, of course, you can call the automobile club for a route. If you want to build a house, you'll probably engage an architect. But, when you write an essay, you must be your own expert. You must make your own plan.

How do you make a plan for an essay? In the same way you would write the essay without one, but in miniature. The hour you would waste in writing three paragraphs you would later reject is a minute or two of delay in altering the plan.

If you found your thesis by working out a circular diagram like those in Figures 2 and 3 (pp. 64, 66) in Chapter Three, you already have a plan that may be nearly sufficient, at least for a short essay. The only lack is order (a serious matter, certainly), which you can supply by numbering the contributory ideas in a sequence that seems logical for the linear development of the thesis. As you do, you will probably reject a few of the ideas as unsuitable and add a few that occur to you in the meantime. If, because of the circular arrangement, you have difficulty establishing even a tentative sequence for linear adaptation, you can transfer the material to a list, rearranging it as you do so and making further adjustments with arrows. Or you can use the material (directly from the diagram, or from the list) to work out an outline. Or you can work out or adapt another diagram more suitable to your needs or taste.

One which works well for many writers looks like a crudely stylized line drawing of a tree. Turn the page sideways; the tree has been cut down and is lying horizontal, and you can write on it normally. Along the trunk you write the thesis. You will determine the number of big branches by the number of major arguments or major points of development. The smaller branches, stemming from the major ones, are for arguments or points subordinate to them. If your essay will support or defend the thesis rather than argue or develop it, your imagination may prefer to consider the same diagram a tree whose branches have been cut off. Your essay is now plotted as a root system, holding up the trunk, your thesis. This diagram, in either consideration you choose to give it, has the advantage of being easily added to or subtracted from: you simply pencil in another branch or root, or lop one off.

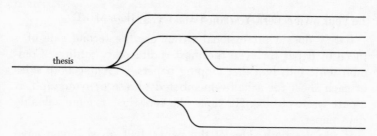

thesis

Figure 8.   Developing an Essay Plan from a Thesis.

## COMPOSE ON THE TYPEWRITER IF
## YOU CAN

You can read your own handwriting well enough; you're accustomed to it; it's personal and comfortable, both to write and to read. The typewritten draft, however, is cold, impersonal, sharp-edged, and rudely frank. Errors that hide in the handwritten page seem to jump out at you from the typed page. You get more words on a page if you type, even triple spacing; thus at a glance you can see much more and save time you might otherwise waste by repeating ideas, shifting tense, or neglecting reference. Later, when you go over a typed page with your pencil to tighten, adjust, correct, or edit it, you'll find your work much easier.

If you are an accomplished typist, you will be able to shoot down your ideas on the wing. You'll work faster, and you'll bag more ideas than you can in handwriting. If you are an average typist, you'll probably need to acquire the habit of thinking and typing at the same time. This habit is one of the most valuable aids to efficiency; it is worth the effort to acquire it.[5] If you are not a good typist, composing on the typewriter is probably not for you. Save that laborious effort for the second draft and for the final version of the essay, if your instructor wants completed assignments typewritten.

## USE ONLY ONE SIDE OF THE PAPER

Rarely does a professional writer use the second side of a piece of paper for even the most rudimentary jottings. Common sense tells him that flipping papers, searching both sides of each sheet for a half-remembered phrase or paragraph, is a pure waste of time. His time, like your time, is more valuable than paper.

If you use both sides of the paper, half of what you have written is hidden when you try to lay out the draft to check your progress against your plan. When you want to reorganize, to move something to another part of the essay, there is

[5] Most average typists who have used the typewriter only for copying what they have written need effort and patience to learn to coordinate their fingers with their thoughts. They should practice when there is no pressure, composing relatively easy things like personal letters or expansions of class notes. When suddenly they realize that they are composing directly, the frustrating hours will seem like a small investment.

nothing to do but recopy if you are not to maim or destroy whatever is on the reverse side. Unnecessary copying is an enormous waste of time.

## LEAVE SPACE FOR REVISION

When you write the first and second drafts, leave wide margins on both sides of the page, and skip lines. If you type, triple space; if you compose in longhand, use only every third or fourth line. You'll be coming back to the drafts with a pencil, to add, make choices, adjust, change, revise. You must leave space to work and rework. Much of writing is rewriting. If there's not space to rewrite, you'll recopy—over and over—and waste not only paper but time.

## USE SCISSORS AND TAPE OR STAPLER

To move a sentence or a paragraph in organizing or reorganizing, to insert a part you forgot earlier, to expand on points insufficiently developed, to replace a passage with a clearer version—don't recopy. Use scissors and transparent tape or stapler. Simply cut the page in two at the proper place, or cut out the portion you've decided to replace, insert the addition or substitution, and fasten it in place with the tape or staples. You'll save yourself time you can use later for polishing the essay or proofreading thoroughly.

## DON'T RECOPY YET

Recopying drains your energy; it cancels alternate versions and commits you to choices you may have made only tentatively. If you write on only one side of the paper, if you leave space between lines and in margins to permit legible changes, if you use scissors and tape or staples for organizational changes, recopying is unnecessary until your paper is close to its final form. Unnecessary copying is only busywork.

## DON'T ERASE, OBLITERATE, OR
## DESTROY ANYTHING—YET

Erase nothing on the first and the second drafts. Erasure is a waste of time and effort, and that which is erased is lost. When you delete a sentence, a phrase, a word, draw a single clean line through it. When you delete a paragraph or consecutive sentences, make an enclosing line and a single X sprawled across the entire passage. Be sure whatever you delete is still legible: you may change your mind later and want to keep it, or simply move it. The finger-numbing pounding out of "mistakes" with rows of typed X's may suitably express your fury or frustration, but it, too, is a waste of time, effort, and perhaps useful material.

In writing, as in few other endeavors, hindsight can clarify foresight. Leave the wherewithal for looking back—and for going back, if necessary. Don't burn any bridges; you may need them, and it's hard to rebuild them from memory.

It is good insurance to file all the notes, plans, and drafts for your essay until the essay is returned to you graded (or even, if you have space, until the end of the term). These are the record of a process. First, you may want or need to review the process in the light of comments on your marked and graded essay. Second, the instructor or grader may ask you to clarify a few points or to submit a revision, and it is good sometimes to retrace a step or two before starting over. If much time has elapsed between the early drafts and the return of your paper, you may have forgotten material that will be plain in the notes and rough copy. Third, of course, there may be your own curiosity to satisfy: "How could I have said *that*?" [6]

[6] There is, furthermore, the chance, small but quite real, that the question of plagiarism will arise. If somehow another student has submitted an essay identical to yours, the contents of your file will establish you as owner, him as thief. If you have written like an angel and the instructor suspects you have written like a published author, the contents of your file will reassure him of your honesty and ability. (This sort of suspicion is a great compliment, ultimately; after the file has cleared away the smoke, you and the instructor are rather proud of yourselves and each other—the teaching and the learning have been marvelously successful.)

# Getting from the First Draft into the Second Draft

## SPREAD OUT THE FIRST DRAFT—
## AND SCRUTINIZE IT

Lay out the pages of your draft side by side, on the bed or floor if there's not space enough on the desk. Arrange the parts in the order your plan indicates. You may need the scissors now, to separate those parts which share the same pages but don't belong together, or you may need both scissors and tape or stapler to join a paragraph or sentence which extends from the bottom of one page to the top of another. Affix the tape or staples in the margin, because they're impossible to write on, and you'll probably be writing in changes between the margins. Don't fasten separate sections to one another yet. You may want to change the order.

Skim over everything you've laid out to review the ideas you've developed thus far and the order in which they proceed.

*Check it against your plan.* Have you developed all the ideas it incorporates? Have you developed them fully enough? If not, your job is waiting. On another sheet of paper, write whatever it is you need. If you're not sure where it belongs, simply lay it among the other parts wherever it seems appropriate at the moment. You can shift it later, and you can fasten it when you're sure.

*Look for gaps in development and leaps in reasoning.* If the essay has fulfilled your plan for it, but something seems wrong now with the development of the thesis, look for gaps between ideas and for corresponding leaps in your reasoning. Check not only the pages of the draft but again, very carefully, the plan. The essay is not only the result of your plan but its reason for existence and therefore the test of its validity and usefulness. If you recognize omissions now, note them down, and make appropriate additions to the draft. (You must fill in the holes; hoping the reader won't notice them or, if he does, won't mind illogical leaps over them is not facing facts.) On your plan, note at least major additions. You'll refer to it frequently, and it should chart your esssay accurately as well as guide your progress on it.[7]

*Review for progression.* Check the order in which you have presented ideas. Now that they are extended, expanded into sentences and paragraphs, do the ideas follow one another as well as you thought they would? Do they build to a climax, a point of highest interest? Is the line of reasoning orderly? Or does it seem to jump ahead and then backtrack?

If you're satisfied, you can proceed with the tape or the stapler to make the pieces of your first draft hold still in the proper order for further work with your pencil—for crossing out and writing in; for tightening and polishing.

## ADJUST THE PLAN AND THE ESSAY
## TO REALITY

But perhaps you're not satisfied, though you planned carefully and worked accordingly. Check the plan. It may have flaws not evident before the first draft is finished. As you follow a plan, you are in effect testing it, just as you periodically test the essay by comparing it with your plan for it. Rarely if ever can any writer, in drawing up whatever plans and outlines he needs, predict with utter accuracy every point of his final development. Unless you have a nimble and graphic imagination, or you think in outlines (some people do), or your luck is very good, you can expect to rearrange at least some of the parts more than once.

Plans, outlines, diagrams—all the apparatus of prewriting— are to serve you, not you them. To follow them blindly is to make masters of your servants.

Plans are flexible, and reality is not; it is not only better but easier to adjust a plan than to distort an essay to fit it. '

*Don't be overawed by your plan.* Don't make the essay suffer because you are in awe of your own intentions or unduly

---

[7] In a longer and more complex essay, you may want to expand the plan as you write, to record minor as well as major points of development you had not foreseen.

respectful of your plan. Remember the dimwitted giant Procrustes, who stretched his short guests and chopped the feet off his tall ones to make them fit his guest bed. The bed was there first.

*Don't surrender—regroup.* If you're not satisfied, this is the time to try rearranging the plan and thus reorganizing the essay. This is *not* the time to quit trying, recopy the draft, and hand in what you hope will pass for a well-organized essay. This is *not* the time to tear up both draft and plan and start all over, to devise an entirely new plan.

*Rework the transitions.* In rereading a new arrangement, remember that you're checking how the realigned ideas mesh, not how the essay "sounds." It will probably sound very rough. Don't unthinkingly expect smooth-functioning or even properly functioning transitions. The realignment of pages, paragraphs, and perhaps sentences will make useless and perhaps misleading most of the transitions you made earlier between parts now moved. If the new order is definite, you'll need to check and adjust all specifically transitional terms. For example, a *therefore* must proceed from evidence; you'll make sure the evidence is there, or you'll change *therefore* and perhaps compensate further within the sentence. Be sure you don't have a *furthermore* where you need a *yet*. You'll need to check, too, elements whose transitional function is only secondary, such as pronouns. If, after the cutting and moving and splicing, *she* refers to *United States Army bases* rather than to *the typical enlisted WAC,* make the necessary repairs. Meanwhile, you may discover other minor flaws—a superfluous sentence or paragraph, or an idea in need of more support.

## TYPE THE SECOND DRAFT

If you type at all, it is good to type the second draft—still leaving two or three spaces between lines to allow for final changes, for tightening, editing, and polishing. The clean, widely-spaced lines will help you see clearly where such work is needed as well as give you space for it. They may show you that you must do the more drastic work of shifting sentences or paragraphs again. Don't hesitate; cut and splice as before.

## The Writer's Plague—the Bogdown

Most writers expect to get stuck occasionally. No matter what methods they follow, the bogdown may still occur, if not today, another day. Yet the measures intended to avoid it at least help to postpone it and then, when it comes, to limit its debilitating effects.

### HOW TO AVOID (OR AT LEAST POSTPONE) THE BOGDOWN

*Don't expect to write the essay in one session.* Both you and the essay will suffer if you force yourself to finish it at one sitting. Trying to "get it out of the way" at one time, whether one hour or six hours, you place yourself under too much pressure, intensified, of course, if it is the evening before the assignment is due. In working against time, when you bog down, you become desperate; desperation soon becomes despair.

In history, great feats have been accomplished under pressure. Yet history doesn't record what is not accomplished, except of course spectacular failures. But as you would hesitate to compare your writing an essay with a brilliant coup or an act of great courage, so would you find the term "spectacular failure" inappropriate for a botched or inept essay. The much-admired ability to work under pressure is usually in reality the ability to relax under pressure, to work well in spite of pressure. Pressure overcomes inertia, it is true; but waiting for time to pass, pressure to build, and tension to generate within yourself and drive you to work is preferring bondage to freedom, slavery to mastery. On the other hand, self-discipline is a kind of internal pressure you control and apply when you will.

*Don't let ideas escape.* Keep a little pad of paper within reach for incidental jotting.

Just as, when you're writing, the right idea doesn't always come at the moment you need it most, too often one arrives that you're not yet ready for or that you don't need at all for the essay you're working on. It intrudes, perhaps with all its relatives and friends and associates, when you're busy with other ideas. No idea is to be spurned. But to entertain it at such a time is to neglect the others, which may leave and have to be coaxed back later. Put it down on the little pad and let it wait its turn. Then tear off the page and slip it under the pad, which is now ready for the next uninvited idea.

After you've practiced this pad keeping for a few days, you'll find yourself putting tangential ideas down out of the corner of your concentration, as it were, while most of your conscious mind continues with the work in progress. You'll find recorded on the note pages evidence that you have more ideas than you need, evidence to reinforce your faith in your mind's fertility. This jotting has a kind of purgative effect, too: you've done something, however absent-mindedly and hastily, about an intrusive idea; you've disposed of an annoyance; you've cleared your conscious mind for the work at hand. (At the same time, paradoxically, the small act of jotting it down will help file this idea firmly and accurately in your memory for eventual reference.) This method of dismissing one kind of distraction will of course improve your ability to concentrate and therefore help you to write efficiently.

Later, of course, when you have time, you'll leaf through these slips of paper, and you may be pleased with what you find on them. An idea you put down hurriedly may be of great importance now, in the stage your essay has reached. Another may reinforce a rather shaky argument you've already made. Still another may develop into an entirely new thesis or the support of one, for an essay still unassigned. Perhaps one of the notes will be only a reminder to buy potato chips—but how much better than forgetting them, or being distracted from your writing by thoughts of them.

*Don't force yourself to begin at the beginning.* Paragraphs and sentences (and even words) are often called "the building blocks of writing." The analogy between building and writing can be helpful, but it is easy to carry it too far. People (teachers, especially) talk about structure, about building sentences, about laying foundations in the thesis, or on facts; they call an outline a framework. The word *architectural* seems to describe quite nicely the organizational effect you aim for in writing. It is a pleasant, though no doubt overused, adjective that sooner or later almost all critics apply to "well-constructed" novels, symphonies, furniture, sculpture, girls. The entire terminology is not only rather pleasantly appropriate; it is almost impossible to avoid. Thus it is only natural many people forget that its appropriateness is only analogical, merely metaphorical.

An essay is not a building. Thus, assuming you can envision your essay, it's really your own affair if you write the roof first and the basement last. (Sooner or later, you will of course assemble the parts in a logical arrangement according to their functions and relationships each to each.) And the blocks? Polish them last. Then the leftover blocks, the discarded blocks, you needn't bother to polish at all.

So you need not begin writing your essay at the beginning. And it may be better not to. For most people, the most difficult sentences to write are those two or three or four introductory ones, that should be sharp enough to catch the reader's attention, convincing enough to hold it, broad enough to carry the thesis, and strong enough to govern its development in subsequent paragraphs. Besides, striking the right balance between saying too much and not saying enough is not easy.

For many people, those two or three or four sentences seem to grow to six or seven or eight. There is a tendency to overdo the introduction out of fear that the reader will miss the point. There is a twin tendency to overdo the conclusion to make sure he has not missed the point in spite of everything.

You, of course, have the hypothetical reader. He can help you decide how much to tell in the beginning and how much to reiterate in the end. But the decision will be easier when you can read what you have said in the middle. Why not begin with a less demanding task?

A suggestion many fiction writers follow is to pick up a story as you would a kitten, a little in front of the middle. Try starting your essay there. You may discover later that what you first thought of as the beginning of the middle is really the beginning of the essay. If not, you will have the feel of the job by then, and it will be much easier than before to tackle the introduction.

*Ignore the old axiom "Finish one thing at a time."* To disparage this time-honored rule may seem to praise anarchy. But the rule has always had exceptions: even the worst cook will not delay preparing the meat until the potatoes are ready for the table; the entire meal would never be ready—or fit for human consumption.

If you try to put the finishing touches on your first paragraph before you begin to write the second, you may become so involved that you forget what you intended to say in the second. Or you may find that the end of each paragraph will have such finality about it that it seems to conclude the essay, that beginning each subsequent paragraph will seem like adding a postscript, an afterthought. Even if the result is a series of good paragraphs, they will seem unrelated. You'll find they aren't finished after all, for you'll have to make changes to provide for transition from one to another.

The process of finishing one thing at a time leads to a premature feeling of "doneness." The goal becomes finishing a paragraph rather than an essay. You will let down as you finish each paragraph and have to force yourself to set up a new goal before you can get to work on the next. Unless you are very resolute, finishing one thing at a time may mean not finishing at all.

*Overwrite.* When the ideas and the words are flowing, don't do anything to slow them down. This is the time to produce content, not apply rules. If, while you are composing the first draft, you try simultaneously to apply every rule and every prescription you've ever learned, you'll be concentrating on them rather than on the ideas, and the essay will suffer.

Don't worry about being wordy, or redundant, or repetitious, or ornate. Don't worry about the mixed metaphor or the overloaded sentence. It is much easier later to tighten your essay than to expand it. And expansion at later stages all too often is only plumping or padding.

*Don't make minor choices now.* Writing involves choosing. You choose the subject, the idea, the thesis, and all the parts of their development. You choose not only one word but the place to put it, which is itself the result of a series of choices and which in turn influences the choice of each word. Yet if, in composing the first draft, you allow yourself to concentrate on a minor decision (a choice of phraseology or of sentence form), you can easily bog down.

Furthermore, in the heat of production, it is almost impossible to be a cool and disinterested judge. The choices you make now you may well revise later anyway. Leave them until later.

If several possibilities of phrasing come into your mind when you need only one, put them all down rather than sit and compare their merits or consider the appropriateness of each in a context that isn't all there yet.

You will probably evolve your own system of putting down alternatives in such a way that you can choose later. Figures 9 and 10, on page 116, illustrate the same fragment of a first draft in two physical versions, both of them clear and easy to rework. Notice that the student writer has not bothered to finish one unfortunate sentence or to discriminate between more and less worthy phraseology elsewhere. He is depending on his good sense to help him later. Now his good sense tells him to keep on going.

Writing the first draft is a little like driving a car through deep snow. If you hesitate, you lose momentum. If you stop, when you try to start again the wheels will spin, but you'll probably stay in the same place.

Satchel Paige once said, "Don't look back. Something might be gaining on you." When you are writing, time is gaining on you. Only when you're finished with the first draft is it safe to look back.

The inventor
The would-be inventor
The free-lance inventor must have and keep an open mind. He
becomes aware of a need, perhaps an undefined one,
learns about                 perhaps one no one else has noticed
                                                realized,
perhaps one many people have known of for a long time. He thinks
                        complained   some time.   ponders
                                        years.
about it
over it until it, or a part of it, forms itself as a fairly
                        emerges        rather specific
problem. Now all he has to do is solve the problem. He keeps
thinking, and he draws up many plans for possible solutions
pondering                                 tentative answers,
out of one of which he can develop his invention.
His invention will be a machine
                something   ,
                        a device that no one else has ever made before
Because no one else has even seen this machine
            the idea and the understanding of the specific problem
Because it is his own idea, no one can help him very much. Probably
he will have to make all the parts for the device himself
                        his own parts himself           and assemble
them himself, and if they do not fit he must redesign them
                                work                     or try
other materials.
            metals. Yet as he does all this himself—fits, welds, links,
joins, adjusts, eliminates, replaces—he must think of other people
besides himself. He must keep them and their needs and the effects
it
his invention
the new device will have on them always before him. He aims toward
particular effects, it is true. Yet sometimes the effects he aims for are
not always the ones he gets, and he must be alert to other possibilities
possibilities.
other than those he intends
                        anticipates. Perhaps the device which he
intended
expected to revolutionize
            revitalize
            rehabilitate old trolley lines will only make ski lifts
run more efficiently but do nothing at all for old trolley lines. If

he is open-minded
    wise
      sensible, he will adjust his plans
            change his sights
                  aims, adjust his plans, alter his
solution, consider another group of people
                customers
      public.
      market.

Figure 9.

The inventor/ would-be inventor/ free-lance inventor must have and keep an open mind. He becomes aware of/ learns about a need, perhaps an undefined one/ perhaps one no one else has noticed/ realized, perhaps one many people have known/ complained of for a long time/ some time/ years. He thinks about it/ ponders over it until it, or a part of it, forms itself/ emerges as a fairly/ rather specific problem. Now all he has to do is solve the problem. He keeps thinking/ pondering, and he draws up many plans for possible solutions/ tentative answers, out of one of which he can develop his invention. His invention will be a machine/ something/ a device that no one else has ever made before/ Because no one else has ever seen this machine/ the idea and the understanding of the specific problem/ Because it is his own idea, no one can help him very much. Probably he will have to make all the parts for the device himself/ his own parts himself and assemble them himself, and if they do not fit/ work he must redesign them or try other materials/ metals. Yet as he does all this himself—fits, welds, links, joins, adjusts, eliminates, replaces—he must think of other people besides himself. He must keep them and their needs and the effects it/ his invention/ the new device will have upon them always before him. He aims toward particular effects, it is true. Yet sometimes the effects he aims for are not always the ones he gets, and he must be alert to other possibilities/ possibilities other than those he intends/ anticipates. Perhaps the device which he intended/ expected to revolutionize/ revitalize/ rehabilitate old trolley lines will only make ski lifts run more efficiently but do nothing at all for old trolley lines. If he is open-minded/ wise/ sensible, he will adjust his plans/ change his sights/ aims, adjust his plans, alter his solution, consider another group of people/ customers/ public/ market.

Figure 10.

*Circle doubtful words.* While you're stopped to check the antecedent of a pronoun, or to look in the dictionary for the spelling or the definition or the usage of a word, or to leaf through the thesaurus for the "perfect" synonym, you may be settling into a bogdown. When you're in doubt about a word, circle it with a quick movement of your pencil and keep going. If you can't think of the word you need, circle the empty space, or slash a dash, and keep going. Later, you can look back, and the circles will remind you to look things up. Later, the word—or a better one—will come, or you can find it.

*Don't be a perfectionist—yet.* When you are tempted to stop and polish a sentence until it sparkles, remember that the assignment was not to write a beautiful sentence but to write an essay. This sentence can't exist in a vacuum, and, perfect though you may make it, it can't exist for its own sake. Its purpose, like that of all your other sentences, is to help convey the burden of your thesis. It has obligations of meaning to the sentences on either side of it and to the paragraph in which it will work, as well as to the essay as a whole. It must fit into the essay, not the essay around the sentence.

But, were the latter the case—and it emphatically is not— if, say, your total output for half an hour is that one sentence, can you expect to provide even an adequate setting for it within the remaining time you've allotted to the assignment?

It's inevitable that you will need to give more time to some sentences than to others to make them clear, and it's more than likely that you will want to give extra attention to certain sentences whose meaning will have strategic importance in your essay. But the time to do such work is not now. There's always a chance that the sentence you spend so much time polishing now will be one you delete later for reasons quite apart from its style. But there is another reason for not being a perfectionist yet.

For example, you have written a sentence so obviously clumsy you knew as you were finishing it something was wrong. The sentence to follow is half formed in your mind. Yet you look back, and the sentence does indeed look bad. Half an hour later, you finally have the best sentence for your purpose. What purpose was this, especially in relationship to what was to follow? What in the world *had* you intended to say after this one? That half-formed sentence which would have followed—even the idea of it—has retreated. You must pursue it, but it is gone. You look at the wall. No, it's not there—it has escaped. You have bogged down.

## WHAT TO DO IF YOU DO BOG DOWN

If you do bog down, if your pencil can move no farther, if you can't possibly think of another thing to write—but you know you haven't finished the essay—don't despair. Remember that practically all writers bog down at some time or other, many of them at some point in practically every piece of writing. Why should you be the exception? The bogdown is temporary, not permanent. Other writers pull themselves out. And you can. To quit now, to tear up what you have written, to start wearily all over again with another subject, is only to punish yourself for being human. Work yourself out of the bogdown by doing now some of the lesser but important tasks that you'd have to do sooner or later anyway.

*Become your hypothetical reader.* Assume the role of your hypothetical reader and, through his eyes, from his point of view, read everything you have written so far. Ask the questions he would ask. Remember, he knows something about the subject, but not so much as you do. He is the intelligent layman; you are the specialist. Have you filled in for him sufficient background for the understanding of your line of reasoning? Have you told him everything he needs to know? Have you told him everything you want him to learn? How well have you told him—how clearly? Might he misunderstand something you've said because it is undeveloped, or vague, or ambiguous? Is there any break in your reasoning, where he might lose his way?

Remember that he is sophisticated. He is aware of all the old devices that pass for thinking. He has heard all the hackneyed mouthings that pass for communication. Are any of your statements mere platitudes, expressions old and outworn yet presented as if they were new and important? Are they clichés, expressions once bright and strong but now dull and weak from overuse? Are they truisms, so well known that they do not bear repetition? Are they commonplaces, obvious and conventional?

If your essay argues, remember that your hypothetical reader is of the opposite conviction. He is not merely a skeptic but an opponent, yet an opponent you wish not so much to devastate as to win over to your own camp. If your essay attempts to persuade, he is not easily led: he has more than a normal share of inertia; perhaps he is a bit stubborn; perhaps he is already devoted to an opposite persuasion. (For example, if your essay urges a return to the center city, he is a suburbanite—confirmed, or enthusiastic, or at least contented.)

The better you understand the opposition, the better equipped you can be to meet it. Become a spy in the enemy camp: observe your own defenses from the enemy's point of view. Where are they weak? Where is your essay vulnerable? Where should you strengthen it?

Ask yourself also, "What would my hypothetical reader—my opponent—do if he were trying to convince me or persuade me to join his side?" Assume his role, and jot down any arguments *he* could make. You may be discouraged to find that much can be said for his side. Simply consider him, then, a more worthy opponent than you had expected. A few weapons don't necessarily make him invincible. After all, if there were nothing to be said from an opposing view, no one would hold it, and there could be no argument. You'd be beating a dead horse in writing this essay, trying to whip a dead issue into action—saying the obvious, saying nothing that needs saying.

So proceed to refute the arguments you have found for the hypothetical reader. Explain how each one is (*if* it is, of course) false, or exaggerated, or falsely based, or fallaciously arrived at, or contradictory of one of his other arguments, or less important than it seems, or unimportant because another argument counterbalances it, or irrelevant, or less relevant than a point *you* can make.

You may find that you can't deal effectively with all his arguments as you have found them. To ignore them, to pretend they don't exist, is to leave your paper too vulnerable. Assume his role again, and expand his arguments. It is in the extension of it that an idea shows flaws or weaknesses not otherwise evident.

Thus perhaps the best way to write a really strong argumentative or persuasive essay is to write—or at least plan carefully—two: the first from the point of view that opposes yours and the second from your own, which systematically (point by point) refutes the first, besides presenting your own case and the arguments for it. The first "essay," of course, you do not hand in; therefore you needn't bother to organize it well, to phrase it carefully, or to polish it. A simple outline may be all you need. You must, however, be careful not to write the second as if your reader has already read the first. Your hypothetical reader is looking over your shoulder only hypothetically.

Usually, after a thorough investigation of an opposing view, you find that you understand your own much better than before. You find reasons for believing what you hitherto only felt. An opinion becomes a studied, logically arrived-at judgment. On the other hand, it is quite possible you will prefer the opposing view, once you understand it, to the one you originally held. You may realize that the other side of the fence is where you belong, once you've been there. In this case, it is logical to go there, and what a formidable opponent you will be for those of your former persuasion if you don't forget the views you formerly held.

Your hypothetical reader will stir you to action, mental and verbal. He's not a dummy sitting on the other side of your desk and grinning at you. He is that half of your own potential you may never otherwise discover.

*Look up the circled words.* While you were writing the first draft, you didn't have time to look up words you were unsure of. Do this job now.

Check the spelling of the words you circled. Make check marks inside the circles of those words you've spelled correctly and of those misspelled words you've corrected; you'll know how far you've gone if you're interrupted, and there's also a pleasant sense of accomplishment in checking off completed work. Take a good look at the recommended pronunciation of the words you've misspelled. You may have been slurring or omitting the sounds of some letters or even adding some letter sounds as you spoke those words. Often a quite innocent mispronunciation or even a regional pronunciation is responsible for an error in spelling.

Check the definitions of the words you circled. To be sure each word means exactly what you want a word in that context to mean, read the full dictionary entry carefully, including the advice on usage and any examples of its usage. All college dictionaries list synonyms for many words. Go through these when you find them, and perhaps run down the definitions of a few synonyms, to make sure you have the precise word for the precise job.

*Make some choices.* This is a good time to make some of the minor decisions you didn't stop for when you were rushing ahead with the first draft. Now that you're stopped anyway, you can consider the list of five adjectives where you want one, choose the one most suitable to your intentions and the context, and cross out the others—leaving them still legible, in case you should want to reconsider.

*For precision and clarity, weed out the overwriting.* If you've followed the advice earlier in the chapter, you have probably said more than you need to say on at least a few points. And some passages are probably too voluminous for the meaning they convey. Look back now. Find the overemphasis, the useless repetition, the empty phrases some of your sentences may be loaded with.

Try not to be appalled at the lack of restraint some sentences may reflect. You may be tempted to throw everything away. Don't, for you'll be throwing away the good with the not so good. If you start all over in such a state of mind, you may well produce a sterile, inert essay, and you'll be hard put trying to infuse it with life.

Think of the overwritten passages as luxuriant rather than rank. Think of weeding them out, perhaps trimming them, not of chopping them down.

As you do this work, keep in mind that you have two principal obligations, one to yourself and one to your reader. The first is precision. Your finished essay—and every part of it— should say exactly what you intend it to mean, neither more nor less, not approximately, not a little to the left or a little to the right. If you want a passage to convey excitement, don't let it sound hysterical. Don't assume that your reader will guess he is to get a melancholy effect from a maudlin passage. The second obligation is clarity. Oversimplification can distort your meaning just as unnecessary complexity can obscure it. But always think of precision first, then of clarity, or you may be making quite clear something you don't intend at all. Sacrifice neither for the sake of simplicity or economy. These are certainly desirable effects, and they are useful means, but they are not ends in themselves.

Assume the following is an example of your ordinary first-draft overwriting:

> The city fathers worked heroically, faithfully, day after day, evening after evening, in and out of scores of public meetings to insure the passage of the tax levy that was so necessary, so vital to the welfare, the very life of the community.

When you return to this sentence, you recognize the overkill immediately. *Heroically* isn't the best word to describe what must have been merely hard work; if you were to keep it, you'd have to include information to make it credible. You don't want *faithfully;* you haven't said what the city fathers were being faithful to. *Day after day* and *evening after evening* overlap. The city fathers would have worked (*spoken?*) at meetings, not *in* meetings. But that pleasant little *in and out of* would be *at and out of*. Can you say *at and away from?* You don't like that, either. How were the city fathers working when they weren't at meetings? And *scores* of meetings? How many, really? Whose meetings? Realizing you've opened a Pandora's box of questions of *where* and *how* that you'd need an extra paragraph to answer, you decide to omit this part of the sentence, since it serves no larger purpose in your essay. (If it did, of course, you couldn't evade the problem, and you'd probably develop this single sentence into a paragraph or two.) The last part of the sentence is easier to weed out. Because of the appositive structure, you have a classic redundancy in *vital to the life*. For the same reason, you have *necessary to the life of the community*, an obvious exaggeration: without the tax, the community would probably not die but muddle along somehow. You won't need such a long conclusion now, because the sentence won't be so long as it was. You pull out all the weeds. Now you have this sentence:

> The city fathers worked day after day to insure the passage
> of the tax levy that was so vital to the welfare of the com-
> munity.

You know· this is much better than the first version, but your
hypothetical reader suddenly sneers and asks a few questions
such as " 'So vital' that *what?*" Realizing the sentence isn't so
precise as it might be, you go through it again, making it more
specific this time. The result is an honest, hard-working sentence: though it's only half as long as the first version, it says
more than either the first or the second; it says what you
mean; and it says it clearly.

> The mayor and the commissioners worked hard to convince
> the citizens that without another tax levy the city could not
> remain solvent.

Here's another example, a sentence that may have seemed
marvelously rich and splendid at the time you were writing
it but that now seems only purple:

> This party is organized upon the foundation of the sterling
> American principle that nowhere in this land or any other
> land should anyone, white or black, rich or poor, educated or
> uneducated, ever be deprived of the rightful and equal pro-
> tection of the law.

Stripped of ornamentation, the sentence has the dignity and
strength of simplicity:

> This party is founded on the principle that all men have the
> right to equal protection of the law.

*Doodle words or phrases.* A favorite pastime of the
bogged-down writer is doodling little pictures, scrolls, or geo-
metric designs. Don't let yourself make these beautiful aids to
daydreaming. If you are so deeply bogged down that you can't
help doodling, doodle words and phrases connected with the
subject of your essay. Words are your tools; the subject is raw
material. Almost without realizing, you may produce a new
series of associations and ideas, some of which will be directly
or indirectly useful in developing your thesis.

# The Journal

If you are a serious writer or if you are serious about improving your writing, doubtless the daily journal is the most effective single means of developing skill. The most immediately noticeable benefits of journal keeping are not, however, in the writing; they are a result of it. On the pages of the journal you can spread out your thoughts and examine them, analyze them, clarify your motives, understand yourself. Private writing seems to invite unself-conscious expression. This brings you to increased consciousness of self, increased understanding of yourself in relation to other people, increased awareness of your place in the universe. In keeping a journal, you can learn about yourself.

By keeping an ordinary diary, such as you perhaps kept in high school, you can hardly scratch the surface of your life:

> Late for school again. Lunch with Mary and Francis—admired his beard—heard later he'll get the lead in the play. Wish I'd tried out. Surprise quiz in German. Riding with Lorraine. The old man from across the street fixed the garage door. Homework. T.V.

In a journal, you keep each entry fairly well to a single subject. Each day, choose an event, a bit of news, a thought, or an impression, and dwell on it. The same day that produced the catchall diary entry above might produce a journal entry like one of the following:

> Fräulein looks like a little beaver—her teeth, her round bright eyes, the shape of her head, her smooth, pulled-back hair, her fur coat over her rounded, slightly stooped shoulders and back (she's always cold), her way of looking up. Her legs in their shiny, dark stockings are like wet sticks of wood.

She scolds us for our errors of German pronunciation in her learned English with the interchangeable *v*s and *w*s. She says *"nicht"* continually.

A horse is motion, strength, softness, sadness, joy, sympathy, relief from strife or from boredom. I like to feel the sinews and hardness and braided muscles of a horse's legs, the gristly resilience of his ears, the sponginess of the veins that network the side of his head. I like to put my cheek against the curved moving surface of his neck, under his mane, and move my head so I can breathe the horse smell through the smooth hide and disturb the warmth that has been hoarded in the long pocket between neck and mane.

Mary gets up at five-thirty one morning every week and rides the city bus to the end of the line and back. She carries a huge straw bag with an enormous poppy cut out of red felt and sewed on one side. In the winter she wears a large, floppy-brimmed black felt hat with a rakish feather, a blue cape with a red satin lining. She smiles and says, "Good morning," to everyone who gets on the bus. She takes her weekly ride because she wants those early-to-work people to see a happy, cheerful, friendly person at least one morning a week.

This evening the man across the street saw me struggling with our recalcitrant garage door and came over to help. He asked me if I would get him an oil can and an old piece of cloth. As soon as he oiled the slides, the door ran up and down easily. When he was finished, I could see that he wanted to talk. As we sat on the back steps I learned that he is retired, has no family, owns two cars (one old, one new), and takes weekly dancing lessons at Arthur Murray's—for the exercise.

The journal is the place to rehearse for and review what might otherwise be only a furious inchoate outburst at your roommate; what might otherwise be an exaggerated commitment in a love letter; what might otherwise be a far-fetched, impractical proposal at a meeting. There is, of course, therapeutic value in many such entries: the journal gives you an outlet for the overflow of your anger or loneliness or dreams.

In the journal you can keep a record of thoughts, reactions, events, impressions, people. Years from now you can read it as a personal history, of course. Much sooner, you can use it as a mine for insights and ideas. In a faithfully kept journal you can find material for any number of essays or stories.

Writing every day develops fluency. If writing is a some-time and a perforce thing—if you write only when you must —then even the simplest writing task seems difficult. But writing every day puts you at ease with your skill; it makes you a relaxed writer. Relaxed, you can increase your control over language. Increased control is greater skill.

Once you have begun writing daily in your journal, you'll find yourself looking and listening with greater interest than before. It will seem as if a special part of your mind is recording impressions and storing details for the journal. You'll notice people and things you'd have ignored before. Your sensitivity will increase; your thoughts will reach out further and with greater intensity than before; you will no longer be content with vagueness.

In the journal you write freely and directly—the journal is the only draft. Sometimes a new journal owner is so enthusiastic over his possession or even worried about posterity that he works out his entries on scratch paper, rewrites them, polishes them, and then copies the final versions onto the journal pages. If you have such impulses, resist them, or you will probably not be a journal keeper for long. If the journal is too time-consuming, it will become a burden you'll soon abandon.

You may want to go over earlier entries and make occasional adjustments. This is easier for you and better for your skill than trying to polish the entry you have just completed: the cooling-off which the older writing has undergone will allow you to be objective. Thus you will have practice in editing. You need not, of course, actively search for "mistakes"; don't regard your journal as a series of self-inflicted grammar tests. But often, in casually reading through several pages, you'll become aware of a recurring weakness, illogical construction, cliché, or mannerism. This you'll want to correct, and you'll usually find your subsequent writing quite naturally free of this specific weakness. You probably won't look for it, of course; you'll be making more sophisticated improvements as time goes on. The cumulative effect of journal keeping is stronger, clearer writing by a more versatile writer.

# Outlining

The only justification for an outline is its usefulness to the writer. It does not exist for its own sake but as a means of predicting and avoiding major flaws in an essay. Outlining helps you to keep to the promise of the thesis by including all necessary material and omitting that which is extraneous. It helps you to arrange material logically. It provides a control over the essay during the writing of it. (See also "Plan," p. 101.)

Since you can develop an outline only after you have determined a thesis, materials that were instrumental in developing the thesis will help develop the outline. Certainly, more ideas in defense of the thesis will appear as you examine it, but none of the ideas will marshal themselves in any logical order until you give them purposeful direction.

Most outlines begin as lists of ideas jotted down as a means of remembering them before other ideas push them from the mind. As a consequence, the lists include fragments of sentences, phrases, even single words that may be meaningless to all but the writer. When you have such a list, the next step is to go over it and fill out the items that need to be better identified. At this time you may notice that some seem to lead off on tangents or some do not contribute to the thesis. Get rid of them. Convert each remaining item into a statement, thus beginning to give rudimentary shape to your material. Many of these statements will be "little theses," developing into paragraphs in the final essay.[1] Then check the list for compound sentences. If you find one, break it at the conjunction to make two sentences. In an outline, a compound

[1] Do not, however, assume that these statements must remain in their present form as ready-made topic sentences. Writing an essay is more than "fattening" an outline.

Title

Thesis:

- I.   First "little thesis" (major support for thesis).
    - A.   Support for I.
        - 1.   Support for A.
            - a.   Support for 1.
                - (1)   Support for a.
                - (2)   Support for a.
            - b.   Support for 1.
                - (1)   Support for b.
                - (2)   Support for b.
        - 2.   Support for A.
            - a.   Support for 2.
                - (1)   Support for a.
                - (2)   Support for a.
            - b.   Support for 2.
                - (1)   Support for b.
                - (2)   Support for b.
    - B.   (And so on.)
- II.   Second "little thesis" (major support for thesis).
    - (And so on.)

Figure 11.

sentence causes trouble, because it is really two (or more) headings masquerading as one. When you have done this job, you are ready to set up your outline.

Go through the list carefully, looking for the three or four points that seem to you best qualified to support, argue, develop, defend, amplify, or maintain the thesis. Some items will seem to have an immediate relevance to the thesis. In the essay, these items will probably be the main points, supported in turn by the other items, whose relationship to the thesis is indirect. When you think you have isolated these items in your list, place Roman numerals (I, II, etc., according to how many main points you have) after them. To give yourself room to work, copy each of the headings on a separate piece of paper.

Check your decisions by comparing the three or four headings you have selected to be sure that one heading is not the cause of or the result of any of the others; or that one heading does not merely repeat what another one says, even though in a different way; or that one heading could not be contained in another as support for it.

Concentrating now on the main points headed by "I," search the list for items that support it. Use a simple "go or no-go" process much as an inspector uses a "go or no-go" gauge in a factory. When you think you have found a supporting item for "I," glance quickly at the other items labeled with Roman numerals to be sure that it does not relate more directly to one of them. If it does not, write the "I" beside it and cross it lightly from the list. As an alternate method, cut it from the list with a pair of scissors and tape it, staple it, or merely lay it on the sheet headed by "I." If you choose to lay it on the sheet, you can more easily shift it about until you find its correct position among the other items you will soon cut out and lay there with it. This alternate method, a bit more mechanical than the first, saves rewriting and allows flexibility in any necessary reorganization later. Using the same process, go through the list to find the material most suitable to the development of "II," and so on.

Now go through all the items you have designated as belonging to "I" and decide which most broadly or directly support that main point. Arrange these in "A," "B," or even "C" positions, if you have that many items. The others designated as belonging to "I" should support "A," "B," and so on and will be numbered "1" or "2." (In a very detailed outline you may find supporting points for "1" or "2." If such points appear, list them as "a" and "b" after "1" or "2.")

When you have transferred all the points on your list to the outline pages, you may find you have a "1" without a "2" or an "a" without a "b." If you have only one such supporting idea for any item, combine it with the item it supports, making a complex sentence out of the two. This rule of not having a "1" without a "2" and so on—for it is a rule of outlining—is logical rather than arbitrary, since nothing can be divided into fewer than two parts. Furthermore, if anything is divided into parts, those parts must be mutually exclusive. For example, "I" and "II" must not overlap; and "A" and "B" must not overlap.

When you have all the items transferred from the original

list to the sheets of paper headed by the Roman numerals, it is time to lay out the sheets and check whether their numerical order represents the best logical order. Look for a progression of thought toward the preconceived end. For example, in the sample outline on this page, the writer moves from the simple motivation of the early pioneers (sheer survival) to the much more complex desire of modern man to live beyond the possibilities of a limited environment. The movement from simple to complex parallels the movement toward a preconceived end. In another case, the movement may be from the less important to the more important, or from a minor to a major concept.

Movement in the essay comes about more easily if you study the major divisions of the outline before you position them, hence the suggestion to use separate pieces of paper for them. You are still completely free to move the sections about and to try various combinations, always striving for a movement or progression of ideas and supporting material.

## THE LIMITED ENVIRONMENT

Thesis: Because conquering nature seems so easy, so exciting, and so rewarding, few Americans heed the warnings of the ecologists.

I. The conquest of nature was the necessary first concern of the early settlers.
   A. They looked upon forests and wild animals as natural enemies that must be destroyed if they, themselves, were to survive.
      1. They cut down and burned the trees to get arable land.
      2. They killed wild animals for food and as a means of protecting themselves and their crops.
   B. Because they thought the vast resources of the land were inexhaustible, they acquired the habit of moving on and leaving their problems behind.
      1. The cut-over land could no longer provide materials for shelter and warmth.
      2. The exhausted soil could no longer produce good crops.

II. Although the Industrial Revolution glorified the multiplication of man's power over nature, it ignored the destruction of natural resources.
  A. Lakes and streams became depositories of refuse.
  B. Land laid waste was abandoned.
  C. Industrial smoke and fumes poisoned the air.
III. People give little thought to the necessity of cooperating with instead of conquering what they now know is a limited environment.
  A. Because man loves good food in plenty, he ignores the effects of the insecticides that the grower uses.
    1. Modern insecticides kill efficiently but without discrimination.
      a. Birds that once kept the insect population in balance are either killed or rendered sterile by the deadly poisons intended to kill insect pests.
      b. Beneficial insects are killed along with destructive insects.
    2. Many destructive insects develop strains that are immune to stronger and stronger insecticides.
    3. Contaminated lakes and streams kill fish or make them unfit as human food.
  B. Because man wants to transport things with speed, and people with both speed and luxury, he ignores the toxic effects of present transportation devices upon the atmosphere.
    1. Automobiles, trucks, and planes add huge amounts of carbon monoxide and carbon dioxide to local atmospheres.
    2. Gases that cannot be absorbed or broken down by atmospheric processes have a cumulative effect upon the world's atmosphere.
  C. Because man is fascinated by his sense of power over natural forces, he continues to build and test atomic-energy devices.
    1. He ignores scientific reports of the effects of atomic radiation upon the genes of men and animals.
    2. He ignores scientific reports that the effect of atomic radiation may be cumulative.

Figure 12.   Two Ways of Visualizing Outline Relationships.

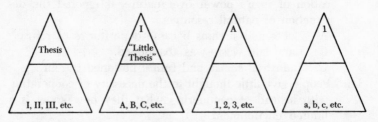

1. **Pyramids**

   The outline suggests a series of pyramidal structures, each consisting of a thesis or a little thesis (or a supporting statement that needs support in turn) at the apex and supporting material at the base.

   In each pyramid only supporting materials directly pertaining to the apex section should be allowed to remain.

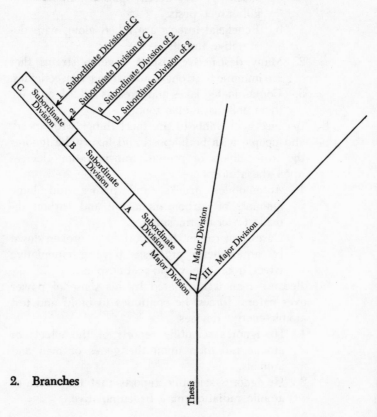

2. **Branches**